BARBARISM

BARBARISM

Michel Henry

Translated by
Scott Davidson

Continuum Impacts

continuum

Continuum International Publishing Group

The Tower Building	80 Maiden Lane
11 York Road	Suite 704
London	New York
SE1 7NX	NY 10038

www.continuumbooks.com

Originally published in French as *La Barbarie*
© Éditions Grasset & Fasquelle, 1987

© Presses Universitaires de France, 2004

This English translation
© The Continuum International Publishing Group Ltd., 2012

British Library Cataloguing-in-Publication Data
A catalogue record for this book is available from the British Library.

ISBN: HB: 978-1-4411-2464-7
PB: 978-1-4411-3265-9

Library of Congress Cataloging-in-Publication Data
Henry, Michel, 1922-2002.
[Barbarie. English]
Barbarism/Michel Henry; translated by Scott Davidson.
p. cm. – (Continuum impacts)
Includes bibliographical references and index.
ISBN 978-1-4411-3265-9 (pbk.) –
ISBN 978-1-4411-2464-7 (hardcover) –
ISBN 978-1-4411-3208-6 (ebook (epub) –
ISBN 978-1-4411-2965-9 (ebook (pdf)
1. Culture. I. Title.
HM621.H46313 2012
306–dc23
2011047165

Typeset by Deanta Global Publishing Services, Chennai, India

CONTENTS

TRANSLATOR'S INTRODUCTION

Michel Henry was a leading French thinker in the latter half of the twentieth century whose writings addressed a wide range of philosophical topics, including phenomenology, theology, economics, political philosophy, ethics, and aesthetics. A good entryway into his work is to begin with his own observation that his thought developed out of an attempt to "understand what I really was." The search for self-knowledge is as old as philosophy itself and has been answered in an astonishing number of ways from Plato's witty answer "a featherless biped" to Aristotle's "a rational animal capable of speech" to Descartes's "thinking thing" and so on, but this effort to "know oneself" gains a new meaning and impetus in Henry's work. His answer to this classical question seems to have been shaped by his involvement in the "Free French Forces" resistance movement in World War II. There he had the experience of having to conceal his true identity along with everything that he truly thought and did. From this experience, he came to conclude that it applies to the entirety of one's existence. One's true identity withdraws from the visibility of the public realm and resides in the secrecy of a clandestine, underground life.

The central aim of Michel Henry's philosophy, from beginning to end, is to articulate the nature and meaning of this invisible aspect of life. It is important, first of all, to note that Henry's conception of life means something altogether different from life in the ordinary sense of the word, where we usually associate life with biology. The study of life thus typically takes its starting point from the study of living beings like plants and animals. Such an approach to life, however, can only ever capture it in a secondary, derivative, and even falsifying way, on Henry's view. This is because it can only grasp the external or outer shell of life, and as a result, it misses its internal aspect. It would be a mistake, however, to take this as a mere rehearsal of the common biological distinction between a phenotype and a genotype, where the genotype would signify the underlying, inner condition for phenotypes that are expressed on the outer surface of an organism.

Both the phenotype and the genotype of a living organism would belong to the external aspect of an organism for Henry, inasmuch as they share the same mode of appearing. They both appear in their separation from the knower who observes them externally and objectively. The collapse of phenotype and genotype into a single mode of appearing establishes the crucial opening for what is entirely novel and distinctive about Henry's own account of life – its break from the biological organism as a model of life.

The distinction between two different modes of appearing emerges as early as his masterpiece, *The Essence of Manifestation* (1963), where Henry develops a radical critique of the history of Western philosophy. Throughout its history, according to Henry, philosophy has been guided by an "ontological monism" that privileges a single mode of appearing and a single mode of being. This charge might come as a surprise, since the history of Western philosophy is usually taken to be a debate between two opposing camps: on the one hand, idealists who reduce the external world to ideas in the mind, and on the other hand, realists who reduce subjective appearances to a mind-independent, external world. The stroke of genius in Henry's account is to show that, in spite of their apparent differences, these two alternatives are actually one and the same. What appears is always conceived in terms of an ek-static object, or in other words, as something that is set apart from and placed in front of the knower. Through his critique of the "ontological monism" of Western philosophy, Henry advocates an altogether different type of appearing. Life in its original essence appears in and through a radical immanence which admits of no separation, no ek-stasis, no mediation, and no representation. Its way of appearing does not take place through the seeing of an external object, either in an intuitive or theoretical sense, instead it takes place through auto-affectivity. Auto-affectivity, which is literally a feeling of oneself, occurs in such a way that this feeling and what is felt are no longer separated from one another, instead they are immediately and directly connected. Life in its genuine sense, then, is revealed through the immediate affective embrace in which one feels oneself to be alive.

This auto-affective experience of one's own life constitutes Henry's answer to the classical question of who we really are. This experience constantly takes place within oneself as long as we are alive, although it usually remains in the background due to the fact that we simply take it for granted and do not pay attention to it. Ultimately, this forgetting of our original essence by individuals and society alike, signifies more than a mere cognitive error. As Henry's practical philosophy shows, its deeper implications extend into all aspects of our everyday lives, including work, economics, education, ethics, aesthetics, religion, and leisure. By spelling out the social, political, and ethical implications of the forgetting of life, *Barbarism* thus comes to play a very important role within the overall development of Henry's philosophy of life, as it helps to show what is really at stake in the more theoretically oriented critique of ontological monism that is the focus of much of his other work.

Though originally published in 1987 and then reprinted in 2000, the shock value of *Barbarism* remains intact even today. The book offers a profound challenge to many of today's most cherished notions – the predominance of the scientific method in the academy, the Enlightenment narrative of social progress through scientific and technological development, the enthusiastic embrace of increased information provided by new forms of media communication, and current trends in education toward a more career-oriented curriculum. Against these notions, the analyses of *Barbarism* develop a powerful counter-narrative that identifies them with a culture of death that seeks the annihilation of life in all its manifestations. The opening lines of the Preface to the second edition provide a clear indication of the general trajectory of the argument: "This book began from a simple but paradoxical realization: that our own epoch is characterized by an unprecedented development of knowledge going hand in hand with the collapse of culture." Through a painstaking analysis of this unprecedented split, Henry traces its origins back to the science of Galileo. The scientific project inaugurated by Galileo consisted of a stripping away of all the subjective features of our relation to objects together with the consideration solely of its objective features that are susceptible to measurement. So, if culture is defined as a product of life and if life is a subjective experience of oneself in the auto-affectivity of life, then it follows that the setting aside of the subjective features of experience entails a setting aside of culture and of one's own life. While this conclusion may be quite benign when it takes place on the theoretical level, it becomes much more vehement and violent when it takes place in the social world, where it implies the annihilation of actual cultures and the actual lives of individuals. The social and political practices that carry out this annihilation of life are what Henry means by the term "barbarism."

Many readers will find special interest in Henry's analyses of the particular practices that are identified with barbarism, and his account of current trends in the university provides an especially good example of this. The encroachment of science and technology across all domains of society has ultimately broken down the walls that previously separated the laws of the university from the rest of society. In so doing, it seeks to extend the same rules to the university that apply everywhere else. This has an impact, as Henry shows, on the two fundamental tasks of the university: research and teaching. Scholarly research signifies a higher form of culture in which life seeks to express and understand itself. But, due to the encroachment of science and technology, it has come to be defined exclusively by the scientific method, which now guides academic inquiry in all domains, including even the humanities. Following the logic of Henry's analysis, the current condition of the humanities is such that they themselves have been transformed into the inhuman. Moreover, the breakdown of the traditional separation between the university and society has had an impact on the instructional priorities assigned to university teaching. Increased emphasis is placed on preparing students for the real world after they graduate. This focus on career-training often goes along with revisions to the university curriculum, with a decrease in the number of hours required in traditional or general education coupled with an increase in the number of hours required in the career track. It is further accompanied by changes in course content, where, for example, in order to make a literature course applicable to real life, students would read newspaper articles about current events rather than the classics. This transformation of the task of education, according to Henry, takes away the critical and creative impulse of the university and reduces it to a mere reflection of the rest of society.

Before moving any further into Henry's argument, it is important to address a facile objection that can all too easily be raised at this point. Based on his criticism of Galilean science and contemporary trends in education, one might accuse Henry of a nostalgia that longs to return to a prescientific world before science and technology. They, to be sure, are not simply detrimental to life but can also be beneficial to it, and likewise to education. While *Barbarism* takes a stand that is largely critical of science and technology, it is important to emphasize that its target is not science or technology as such but the Galilean ideology that enables their predominance. What makes this ideology dangerous, in his view, is that it justifies the encroachment of the scientific attitude onto all other spheres of life, including teaching and research. This is accompanied by a narrowing of the notion of truth, such that the truth becomes reducible to what is scientific and what is scientific becomes reducible to what results from the scientific method. This ideology, which presents the scientific method as the sole source of truth, pits it against all other possible sources of truth, including the life which it eliminates from its analyses.

What Henry challenges is the untethering of science and technology from life, in the pursuit of their own internal logic and development. Henry does not deny the importance or validity of science, but his critique is designed to establish its proper limits. Science and technology are both expressions of culture and life, but they exceed their limits when they forget these origins, turn against culture and life, and set out to annihilate it. The denunciation of barbarism is thus at the same time a call for a renewed spirit of science and technology, one which is aware of its context in life. This renewal of science and technology would occur through an awareness that they originate from life and serve the purpose of life.

In both its initial claims and subsequent development, *Barbarism* is clearly a direct descendent of Husserl's "Vienna Lecture" that was delivered half a century earlier, although Henry never explicitly makes this point. In his own times, Husserl likewise diagnosed Europe to be suffering from a malaise. This spiritual crisis, according to his estimate, could be traced back to the predominance of one mode of rationality – the one found in the natural sciences – to the exclusion of all other forms of rationality. This predominance of the natural sciences produced a deep dissatisfaction in the other cultural forms that were diminished or excluded by it. From this situation, Husserl famously concluded that Europe was faced with a choice between two alternatives:

> There are only two escapes from the crisis of European existence: the downfall of Europe in its estrangement from its own rational sense of life, its fall into hostility towards the spirit and into barbarity: or the rebirth of Europe from the spirit of philosophy through a heroism of reason that overcomes naturalism once and for all.

It is interesting to note, then, that roughly the same alternative is presented in *Barbarism*. That is, either society can continue down the path toward its ultimate self-destruction or it can discover the resources for its spiritual renewal through an embrace of the original essence of life in its genuine sense. Even though the dilemmas presented by the two thinkers present are strikingly similar on the surface, for our purposes it is important to note the key differences between the remedies that they propose.

In response to the European crisis, Husserl called for a return to the original conditions of science and culture in the birth of a "new life-inwardness and spiritualization." On the surface, this call looks similar to the one proposed by Henry, but what this means for Husserl is a return to the lifeworld. The lifeworld points back to an original contact between oneself and the world that precedes the adoption of the theoretical attitude. While Henry's argument moves in the same direction, it ultimately takes a slightly different route. This difference can be located in a slightly different emphasis that he places on the notion of the lifeworld, in French "*monde de vie.*" This slight difference, which makes all the difference, identifies the root cause of barbarism not as a denial of the lifeworld but of the world of life, so to speak. In other words, the way out of the crisis of our time is not to be established through a return to a pre-theoretical contact with the world. For, such a contact still falls under Henry's critique of "ontological monism" that was described above. Instead of renewing our ek-static connection with the world, the "new life-inwardness" to cure the crisis of our time is located in a renewed relationship to life itself. *Barbarism*, accordingly, is Henry's manifesto for life. Its call is for a spiritual renewal that takes place through the reawakening of our intimate, affective connection to the life within us, and perhaps this call is more pertinent than ever in the wake of the current crises from which we suffer today.

While *Barbarism* goes on to pursue in more detail the line of thought outlined above, it is ultimately up to the reader to determine whether or not the proposed remedy has been administered soon enough to cure and, more broadly, whether or not the correct diagnosis and remedy were provided at all. Regardless of how those questions are answered, the deeper and more troubling question that *Barbarism* ultimately poses to its readers is, "Why, in these times of crisis, aren't such questions being asked today?" It is by forcing us to raise that question anew that *Barbarism* remains an essential companion for readers today.

While the above remarks provide an initial orientation for readers approaching this text for the first time, let me conclude with a few technical remarks about the translation. One immediate difficulty has to do with Henry's style, which is made up of sentences that are much more elliptical than English style would allow. To make the translation more reader friendly, I have broken his sentences down to shorter and more direct forms that better conform to the standards of conventional English, but I have retained whatever logical connection was applied between those sentences. Whenever it helped to clarify Henry's meaning, I have also opted to replace pronouns with the nouns to which they refer. The result, I hope, is a text that will be as clear, accessible, and enjoyable to the English-speaking audience as possible, while at the same time preserving the meaning of Henry's text.

Finally, there are a few technical terms employed by Henry that should be noted due to their particular difficulty. Henry describes communication in the modern world as "existence mediatique." Rather than introducing a new term into English, however, I have rendered this with the less dramatic expression "the media world." A similar strategy was used for Henry's use of the term "ivresse," which is a polite way of saying "drunkenness." When used to describe joy, it could be rendered "drunk with joy" or "intoxicated with joy," but these expressions did not work well in the context of the English sentences where they are used and so I have opted instead for the less dramatic expression "height of joy." Finally, an important and interesting term used in this work is "Corps-propriation." This term is an unusual derivation of the French "corps propre," which would usually be rendered "one's own body." This expression just did not fit smoothly into the text, so I have opted for the hyphenated term "Bodily-ownness." Due to my dissatisfaction with the term and the weight it carries in Henry's text, I have included the French term in parenthesis wherever it appears in the text.

PREFACE TO THE
SECOND EDITION

This book began from a simple but paradoxical realization that our own epoch is characterized by an unprecedented development of knowledge going hand in hand with the collapse of culture. For the first time in the history of humanity, to be sure, knowledge and culture are diverging to the point of being opposed in a titanic battle – a struggle to the death, if indeed it is the case that the triumph of the former entails the disappearance of the latter.

This situation is just as dramatic as it is mysterious. It can be clarified by going back to its source at the very beginning of the seventeenth century, when Galileo declared that the knowledge that human beings had always trusted was false and illusory. This knowledge is the sensory knowledge that leads us to believe that things have colors, odors, tastes, and sounds that are agreeable or disagreeable, in short, to believe that the world is a sensory world. But, the real world is composed of un-sensed material bodies that are extended and have forms and figures. Its way of being known is not the sensibility that varies from one individual to another and thus only offers appearances, but the rational knowledge of these figures and forms: geometry. The geometrical knowledge of material nature – a knowledge that can be formulated mathematically (as Descartes demonstrated right afterward) – is the new knowledge that takes the place of all others and rejects them as insignificant.

Galilean science does not just produce a revolution on the theoretical plane; it will shape our world by marking a new historical epoch: modernity. Unlike other civilizations whose conditions were complex, multiple, and irreducible to the sheer play of the intellect – to the point that vague, external schemas lacking any real explanatory power can be applied to them (for example, the organic schema of birth, growth, decline, and death) – modernity results from a clearly formulated intellectual decision whose content is perfectly intelligible. It is the decision to understand, in the light of geometric-mathematical knowledge, the universe as reduced henceforth to an objective set of material phenomena. Moreover, it constructs and organizes the world exclusively on the basis of this new knowledge and the inert processes over which it provides mastery.

If it is a question of analyzing an epoch or a civilization, should not such a task be given to history or sociology? In both cases, the method begins with the empirical facts, and its first task is to establish them. On the basis of these facts, one attempts to recognize correlations that are themselves problematic in the work of continual investigation. This type of knowledge is called *a posteriori* because it is always after experience and is subjected to the process of confirmation, rectification, and refutation. In its struggle against relativism and skepticism, traditional philosophy, since Plato, contrasted it with the knowledge of a higher order: *a priori* knowledge. Instead of being subordinated to experience, this knowledge precedes it and makes experience possible. Kant, for example, considers space and time to be the *a priori* forms of sensibility and thus of our intuition of the world. The result is thatall objects in this world - in spite of their various differences - are given and will be given to us as spatial and temporal objects. Anyone who opens the door to take a run or a walk already knows this, even if they do not think about it.

In the text that follows, I took the risk of considering the Galilean presupposition as the *a priori* of modernity. It then became possible to deduce the essential traits of modernity. The first of these was the inconceivable divergence between knowledge and culture. For this, it suffices to size up the Galilean reduction. To separate the reality of objects from their sensible qualities is also to eliminate our senses, all of our impressions, emotions, desires, passions, and thoughts; in short, all of our subjectivity that makes up the substance of our life. This life as it is experienced in its uncontestable phenomenality - this life that makes us living beings - is thus stripped of its true reality and reduced to a mere appearance. The kiss exchanged by lovers is only a collision of microphysical particles.

If one supposes that life is the sole source of culture in all its forms, it becomes evident that putting it out of play also puts culture out of play. Galilean modernity can no longer offer anything but the terrifying spectacle unfolding right before our eyes: the progressive dismantling of what gives life its meaning (*sa raison de vivre*), in each of the domains in which it is expressed. Since it is rooted in life and its continual movement of coming into oneself, experiencing oneself and thus of growing from the self, culture is the set of pathetic responses that life seeks to bring to the immense Desire that runs through it. This response can only be found in itself. In art, it happens in a sensibility that wants to sense more and to feel more intensely. In ethics, it happens in an action that allows this great desire for growth to take place on its own terms. In religion, finally, it happens in the experience that life has of itself, in this mysterious Basis from which it springs forth and continually embraces itself.

Culture – as the auto-revelation of life in its self-growth – is not just present in the higher forms in every society that draws from its secret source (just as it is absent from our society which situates the principle for its organization outside of life). It also fills the lower strata of the human community, where activity answers to basic needs such as food, clothing, the general production of "goods," and even the concrete relations between members of the community. This is why there are cultures of food, shelter, work, erotic relations or relations to the dead – such relations provide an initial definition of the "human".

In a society understood as a community of the living within life, culture is thus everywhere. Everything has a value because everything is done by and for life. The assessment which life conducts arranges each thing in its own terms; from the outset,it gives rise to the kingdom of ends. This evaluation must itself be valuable. It only has a value because life itself is the supreme value, the sole value from which the other ones follow. Why is life the absolute value and the sole foundation for all other values?

That is what life tries to tell us. Suffering, for example, expresses suffering; it thus carries, in its own flesh, the invincible desire to change oneself. As the phenomenological substance of our life, this is the first assessment-the pathetic motivation for all conceivable action. This motif can be deepened immeasurably and can lead us back to the sources of culture and of life, if we consider suffering in its connection to the primal suffering in which life experiences itself and arrives in oneself - in growth and in the enjoyment of oneself - this intoxication (*ivresse*) of life is the absolute value.

To the contrary, nothing has value, or everything is the same – and this is the time of true nihilism – when the inner becoming of life, all the knowledge connected to it and all the forms of culture expressing it, gives way to the anonymous knowledge of homogenous processes by those who study physics. The most brutal sign of this substitution of death for life is the emergence of a hitherto unknown technology. It is no longer rooted in the subjectivity of living bodies whose "instruments" were only the "extension" of them, but in the impersonal knowledge of these material processes, identifying with them and putting them into play unconditionally by a sort of satanic vow: everything that can be done in the blind world of things must be done, without any further consideration – unless perhaps that of profit. As if economics alone could save us today – even though it too has already substituted abstractions for the real work of human beings. This new technology is essentially purely material and foreign to every ethical prescription; it is what directs the principles behind our now inhuman world.

At the time of its publication in 1987, *Barbarism* aroused a large response but also some virulent critiques. Its tone seemed categorical, its claims too sharp. There was something prophetic about these millennial statements. This complaining about a culture that is on its way to disappearing thinly veiled a nostalgia for the past, an attachment to ideas, modes and means of expression that should perhaps make way for other ones.

That was especially the case for the critique of science that some believed themselves to find in the text. Is not modern science, with its extraordinary discoveries, also a form of culture, indeed the most essential and innovative one today? Yet, science can only be a form of culture on the condition that it can escape from the Galilean presuppositions, namely, that it does not dismiss subjectivity. It cannot dismiss the operations of transcendental consciousness without which there is neither a circle nor a square and none of the "characters" of the language through which Galileo claims to decipher "the great book of the Universe." It cannot dismiss the sensibility without which one cannot encounter the content to which scientific idealities inevitably refer: these flashes on a screen that are interpreted as the collisions of microphysical particles. The supposed critique of science was thus merely an invitation to grasp this point in its full concrete possibility.

Yet, subjectivity cannot be reduced to the noetic activity of transcendental consciousness considered in its intentional relation to the ideal meanings that constitute the "noematic" content to which the Galilean reduction arbitrarily limits the reality or actuality of science. By extending classical rationality, Husserlian rationality can indeed lead every objectivity back to its subjective condition. It remains captured under the dual threats of impersonality and anonymity. It is only when the auto-donation of transcendental consciousness in life, and in it alone, is perceived as the ultimate phenomenological foundation of all knowing and all values that science can be called a form of culture. But this questioning back to the most radical foundation is not carried out by modern science, which remains duped by the objectivism that floods our mindset once life is silenced. This is even less so with the technology that it gave rise to, with its supercomputers dedicated to random calculations for people who usually donot know about theory. There is no "culture of computers".

To reintroduce knowledge into the field of life and to affirm, for example, with Marx that "thought is a mode of life" is to understand that no theoretical problem is ever truly autonomous. The Galilean decision to exclude subjectivity from its field of investigation does not only happen on the intellectual plane: in it, life turns against itself. Behind the shift of knowledge, as its cause or its effect, the major phenomena of self-destruction - those of life as well as culture - emerge. *Barbarism* provided a systematic description of these phenomena which are horrible not only for their content but for the inevitability of their unfolding. This tragic feeling of powerlessness that every cultivated person experiences today in face of the "facts" stems from their rootedness in the *a priori* conceived by Galileo. Philosophy had previously reserved this *a priori* for the knowledge of the True and the Good. This *a priori* knowledge of the True and the Good are really life itself in its pathetic archi-revelation. This auto-revelation gives each person to him or herself and makes each human being into what he or she is. That is what leads the senseless project of excluding life to take on the character of murderous madness!

But life is still there. Nothing has power over the tireless process of its coming into the self. This coming into the self, through the pathetic modes of suffering and enjoymentwhere life grows and expands on its own, gives rise to the immense Energy that is fulfilled or calmed through high forms of culture. If they fall into disuse, the unused Energy is not only a malaise, it gives rise to an irrepressible violence, because its force does not disappear but rather increases and is deployed randomly and aimlessly.

After the diagnosis of *Barbarism*, the phenomena of self-destruction have seen an enormous and violent intensification. This is not only visible in the streets. The nihilistic attack against all values, the defense of everything that is against nature and against life, expresses this even more. With violence, it is the development of technology outside of any norms that takes to the extreme this substitution of blind processes for the benefits of effort and the joy of living.

There is no longer any more room to challenge the omnipresent objectivism of modernity. After the unilateral objectivism of science, there is the media which tears the human being away from him or herself. At every moment, it produces the content that comes to occupy the mind, thereby authorizing an unprecedented and unlimited ideological manipulation that prohibits all free thought and all "democracy". It condemns every interpersonal relation to be reduced to external manifestations, for example, love is reduced to the objective movement of bodies and to photos.

It is up to computers to re-establish "communication". What classical thought called the "communication of consciousness" and what contemporary phenomenology refers to as "inter-subjectivity" – for example, the emotional upheaval through which someone becomes the contemporary of another person – now turns up as the appearance of objective messages on a screen. Just like on highways, on the "information superhighway" one cannot make out a face. In this communication, no one communicates with anyone else, and its content becomes poorer as the speed increases. This communication of information is multiple, incoherent, cut off from any analysis, from any criteria of evaluation, from criticism, from history, from its genesis, and from every principle of intelligibility – it is without rhyme or reason. It is high time to introduce computers into the schools so that they can take courses. The communication of information is similar to the communication that takes place between genes. The "naturalization" of the human being, in all its forms and various guises, is the latest avatar of the Galilean *a priori*. The human being is no different from a thing.

Michel Henry
October, 2000

INTRODUCTION:
WHAT WAS NEVER SEEN

We are entering into barbarism. To be sure, this is not the first time for humanity to fall into darkness. One could even imagine that this sad adventure has occurred many times, and it is with a lump in the throat that the historian or archeologist uncovers the traces of a vanished civilization. But another one always followed. On the ruins of the ancient sanctuaries, new temples were built that were more powerful and refined. The fields that neglected irrigation systems turned into pestilent marshes are one day drained and dried again; a more prosperous agriculture is established. This is how history can be represented in a cyclical form. Each phase of expansion is followed by a phase of decline, but a new advance will take place here or there and carry the development of life further.

This seems to be global. It works in conjunction with the forces within the human being; they lean on and raise one another up. All human activities – economic, artisanal, artistic, intellectual, moral, and religious – go together. Whichever one is privileged by the interpreter, there is a recognition of the simultaneous blossoming of practical, technical, and theoretical knowledge. Their results are called Sumer, Assyria, Persia, Egypt, Greece, Rome, Byzantium, the Middle Age, and the Renaissance. In these privileged "spaces", it was the totality of values that made humanity and all that blossomed at the same time.

What is happening before our eyes is something quite different. Since the beginning of the modern era, we are witnessing an unprecedented development of the knowledge that forms "science" and is worthy of claiming this title. This means a rigorous, objective, undeniable, and true knowledge. It is distinguished from all the approximate and dubitable forms of knowledge, belief or superstition that preceded it by the power of its evidence, proofs, and experiments as well as by the extraordinary results to which it has led and which have revolutionized the face of the earth.

Unfortunately, this revolution is also a revolution of the human being. If the increasingly comprehensive knowledge of the world is undeniably good, why does it go hand in hand with the collapse of all other values, a collapse so serious that it calls our own existence into question? For, if it is not only the face of the earth that has been changed, becoming so dreadful that life is no longer bearable there. Beauty – which humans have elaborated and won over so patiently – is thus shown not only to be connected to the appearance of things but to be an inner condition of this life, one that is both exuded and required by it. Because life itself is attacked, all of its values also falter, not only aesthetics but also ethics and the sacred – and with them, so too the possibility of living each day.

The crisis of culture, which can hardly be denied today, has been the object of more or less suspect analyses. The most commonly accepted "explanation" is the following one: with modern science, knowledge has made huge advances; to this end, it had to be divided into a proliferation of investigations, each with its own methodology, conceptual tools, and objects. It is no longer possible for anyone to master them all, nor some of them or even one of them. The unity of knowledge is at stake, and along with it, the discovery of a principle ensuring the agreement and thus the validity of experiments, assessments in all domains, and thoughts themselves. Our everyday behavior is significant in this regard: to deal with each specific problem, we call on a specialist. But, if this practice turns out to be effective for a toothache or repairing a machine, it still does not provide any broad view of human existence and its destiny. Without such a view, however, it is impossible to decide on what to do in any case, inasmuch as this concerns our own existence and not that of a thing.

With the interpretation of the crisis of culture as the result of the indispensable multiplication of knowledge in obedience to science's desire for rigor and objectivity, one presupposition remains unperceived because it is self-evident: these ways of knowing, as diverse as they may be, constitute the only knowledge possible and the only foundation to rational behavior in all spheres of experience. How is it then that, in place of this suitable and self-assured behavior, one can observe everywhere, in each of the orders of life – sensible, affective and spiritual as well as the intellectual or cognitive – the same uncertainty and the same disarray, not just the shaking of the values of art, ethics or religion, but instead their brutal and progressive annihilation? It is really not just a question of a crisis of culture but of its destruction.

This is how the hyper-development of a hyper-knowledge - whose theoretical and practical tools mark a complete rupture with the traditional knowledge of humanity– results not only in tearing down these ways of knowing as illusions but also of humanity itself. Like the swell of the ocean, all the productions of past civilizations rose and fell together, as if of a common accord and without being disconnected – knowledge produced the good, which produced the beautiful, while the sacred illuminated everything. But here we are faced with something that has never really been seen before: the explosion of science and the destruction of the human being. This is the new barbarism, and this time it is not certain that it can be overcome.

Why and how did a certain type of knowledge, which appeared in the time of Galileo and has been considered since then as the only type of knowledge, follow the path of an identifiable and wholly intelligible necessity that resulted in the subversion of all other values and thus of culture and the humanity of the human being? This is something that can be understood perfectly well, if we have a theory of the essence of all possible knowledge and its ultimate foundation; for this foundation is also the foundation of values, culture, humanity, and all its accomplishments. It is because modern science moves away from this foundation in an extraordinary way that it is unwittingly rushing our world into the abyss. Taking the torch of a strange knowledge that has accompanied humanity forever in hand and allowing it to subsist and then to travel through the cycle of civilizations and spiritualities, we can still, from the edge of this abyss, at least shed a few last glimmers of a light onto it in order to reveal the menace, the great rupture, and the collapse.

1 CULTURE AND BARBARISM

Barbarism is not a beginning. It is always second to a state of culture that necessarily precedes it, and it is only in relation to this prior culture that it can appear as an impoverishment and a degeneration. Barbarism, as Joseph de Maistre says, is a ruin, not a rudiment. Culture is thus always first. Even the coarsest forms of activity and social organization, those attributed to primitive groups, for example, are already modes of culture. They have an organization, with implicit laws and types of behavior that all serve to make the existence of the group and its survival possible. Even when these elementary forms seem to be fixed and their blind transmission merely results in the renewal of continually repeated structures, profound forces are at work in order to maintain not only the current state of affairs but also the continuation of life. It could be said that they stand on the lookout. They are not content just to preserve what is the case, instead they wait, with a patience lasting for centuries, for the opportunity to have an impact on these acquisitions and to achieve a new leap, to discover still unperceived relations, to invent a tool or an idea, and to give rise to a new world.

What then is culture? Every culture is a culture of life, in the dual sense whereby life is both the subject and the object of this culture. *It is an action that life exerts on itself and through which it transforms itself insofar as life is both transforming and transformed.* "Culture" means nothing other than that. "Culture" refers to the self-transformation of life, the movement by which it continually changes itself in order to arrive at higher forms of realization and completeness, in order to grow. But if life is this incessant movement of self-transformation and self-fulfillment, it is culture itself. Or at least it carries it as something inscribed in it and sought by it.

What life are we speaking about here? What is this force that is continually maintained and grows? It is not in any way the life that forms the theme of biology and the object of a science. It is not the molecules and particles that the scientist tries to reach through microscopes and whose natures are developed through multiple procedures in order to construct laboriously a concept of them that is more adequate but still subject to revision. The life studied by biologists is thus one that will never be known completely, except in a way that is ideal and as such never attained by scientific progress. Even if we still only have an imperfect notion of biological life today, it should be noted that humanity has survived for millennia without having the least idea of it and without suspecting its existence – *without the changes of human life, its maintenance, its growth and its culture, owing anything to it.* We can thus already anticipate a first truth which it is useful to reflect on at the end of the twentieth century, namely, that *culture originally and in itself has nothing to do with science and does not result from it in any way.*

The life that we are speaking about cannot be confused with the object of scientific knowledge, an object for which knowledge would be reserved to those who are in possession of it and who have had to acquire it. Instead, it is something that everyone knows, as part of what we are. But how can "everyone" – that is, each individual as a living being – know what life is, except in the respect that life knows itself and that this original knowledge of the self constitutes its own essence? Life feels and experiences itself in such a way that there is nothing in it that would be experienced or felt. This is because the fact of feeling oneself is really what makes one alive. Everything that has this marvelous property of feeling itself is alive, whereas everything that happens to lack it is dead. The rock, for example, does not experience itself and so it is said to be a "thing." The earth, the sea, the stars are things. Plants, trees, and vegetation are also things, unless one can detect in them a *sensibility* in the transcendental sense, that is to say, a capacity of experiencing itself and feeling itself which would make them living beings. This is life not in the biological sense but in the true sense – *the absolute phenomenological life whose essence consists in the very fact of sensing or experiencing oneself and nothing else* – of what we will call subjectivity.

Now if we want to say that this extraordinary property of experiencing oneself is knowledge and indeed the deepest form of knowledge, and thus that life, as alive, is this original knowing, as is also said with respect to the knowledge of science, it is important to clarify what sort of knowledge is in question in these two cases and how they are distinguished from one another. Otherwise, the debate over culture and barbarism – which are held together in an essential relation (positively or negatively) to knowledge in general –will become lost in confusion.

Scientific knowledge is objective. But, two things are meant and usually confused by this. First, "objective" can mean that scientific knowledge is rational, universally valid and as such recognizable by everyone. It is true knowledge in contrast with the changing opinions of individuals, particular points of view and everything that is only "subjective." This claim to overcome the particularity and relativity of the "subjective" must be grasped in its full significance. Far beyond a mere rejection of individual differences, it goes back to the deep nature of experience and the human condition and can only be understood on that basis. It played a key role in Galileo's time in the birth of modern science, that is, the mathematical science of nature.

The world is given to us in sensible, variable, and contingent appearances that form only a Heraclitean flux – a river in which one can never bathe twice – in which nothing remains and there is no fixed point for solid knowledge. According to this Galilean science of nature that came to revolutionize the European way of thinking and that shaped it into being what it is, it remains possible to go beyond the relativity of subjective appearances and to display a true being of the world, a world in itself. The knowledge of this world is possible, if one abstracts the sensible qualities and, in a general way, everything that is derived from subjectivity, and if one only retains, as truly existing, the abstract forms of the spatiotemporal world. These forms lend themselves to a geometrical determination that is the same for every mind. In place of individual impressions and the changing opinions they give rise to, a univocal knowledge of the world, of what truly exists, is offered.

The sphere of subjectivity – sensations, opinions, personal thoughts, etc.; in short, everything that can be called the world of the mind or human spirituality – is based on this nature whose true being is proven and ultimately explained by science. The "sciences of the mind" or, as they are called today, the "human sciences" thus do not have any autonomy. They are not symmetrical with the natural sciences. Their studies seem provisional, sooner or later to give way to another type of knowledge, one that will abandon mental reality, that is, the level of human experience, and be directed toward its hidden bases: the world of molecules and atoms. If this domain of human spirituality were the object of culture, it would be with good reason that it would continue to regress to the benefit of more appropriate disciplines. Those might be called the foundational sciences.

One cannot pass over in silence the extraordinary reversal carried out by Husserlian phenomenology of the well-known theses that support the scientific and positivist ideology of our times.[1] The geometrical determinations to which Galilean science seeks to reduce the being of things are themselves idealities. Instead of being able to explain the sensible, subjective, and relative world in which our everyday activity takes place, they necessarily refer to this lifeworld. It is only in relation to it that they have a sense. They are constructed on the inescapable ground of this world. From this point of view, the Earth is not a planet that turns around the sun in the theoretical constructions of science but the ground of every experience to which scientific idealizations inevitably refer. Here one must reiterate the outrageous verdict of Husserl and agree with him that "the arch-originary Earth does not move."[2]

Moreover, the geometrical and mathematic determinations used in the sciences are idealities and thus presuppose the subjective operation that produces them and without which they would not exist. Number, calculation, addition, subtraction, straight, and curve do not exist in nature. They are ideal meanings whose absolute origin is found in the consciousness that creates them in the strict sense of the word and that should be called a transcendental consciousness with regard to them. If geometrical and mathematical idealizations come from subjectivity, this does not reduce them to being mere appearances. Instead, here the world of science finds the principle that continually engenders it and that remains its permanent condition of possibility.

To the extent that the world of the mind, with its own laws and creations, seems to depend on nature – on a human or animal body – this nature is precisely not the world of science with its abstract idealities. It is the lifeworld – a world which can only be accessed within a sensibility like ours and which is only given to us through the endless play of its constantly changing and renewed subjective appearances. Galileo's illusion, like all those who came after him and considered science to be absolute knowledge, was to have taken the mathematical and geometrical world, which provided univocal knowledge of the real world, for this real world itself, is the world that we can intuit and experience only in the concrete modes of our subjective life.

This subjective life does not just create the idealities and abstractions of science, as with all conceptual thought in general. It gives form to this lifeworld in the midst of which our concrete existence unfolds. Something as simple as a cube or a house is not just a thing that exists outside of us and without us, as if it were on its own as the substrate of its qualities. It only becomes what it is due to a complex activity of perception that goes beyond the succession of sensible givens that we have of it and posits *the* cube or *the* house as an ideal pole of identity to which all these subjective appearances refer. Each perception of a side of a cube or a façade of the house refers to the potential perceptions of other sides that have not yet been perceived, following an indefinite play of relations. The same holds for every object in general and for every transcendent formation. Each time, their existence implies a synthetic operation of transcendental subjectivity.

To be sure, in our daily life we do not pay attention to this consciousness that constitutes the world of our usual environment. We perceive the house and are inattentive to our perception of the house. We are conscious of the world but never conscious of our consciousness of the world. It is the task of philosophy to give proof of this tireless activity of the consciousness that perceives the world, conceives the idealities and abstractions of science, imagines, remembers, etc. It thereby produces all of the irreal representations that continually accompany us in the course of real life.

It is true that some scholars have called into question the very existence of this consciousness that classical philosophy placed at the heart of science and of all knowledge in general, first and foremost the sensed knowledge of the world around us. The founders of behaviorism demanded to be "shown" this supposed consciousness in the same way as the other sciences are able to show, in their test tubes or microscopes, the objects of consciousness about which they spoke.[3] They do not realize that consciousness really is this power of "showing" to which they themselves, the other sciences, and every other form of knowledge constantly appeal.

If one were to ask about this consciousness whose transcendental operations constitute the objects of the world of perception before creating the idealities of the scientific world, one must first observe that the power in question is the same in both cases, in the most simple and immediate perception as in the most developed scientific regard: it is the power of showing, of making visible, of putting something into the condition of presence. This making visible is itself a putting-in-front (*faire-venir-devant*) in the condition of the object, such that the visibility in which each thing becomes visible is nothing other than objectivity as such. Objectivity is the foreground of light in which everything that shows itself to us is shown – whether it is a sensible reality or a scientific ideality. Consciousness is traditionally understood as the "subject," but the subject is the condition of the object, which means that things become objects for us and thereby show themselves to us so that we can know them.

This implicit conception of consciousness –that is, of the phenomenality of phenomena – is in the background of most philosophies as well as science itself. Kant, for example, attempts to demonstrate the possibility of experience, and it seems that this possibility belongs to objects, that is, to the set of conditions (the intuitions of space and time and the categories of the understanding) through which objects can be given to us and consequently through which we are able to relate to them and experience them. In Husserlian phenomenology, this possibility of relating to objects, of going out toward them in order to reach them, is intentionality. Intentionality defines the basis of consciousness itself, its power of showing and displaying, or in other words, phenomenality itself. It is quite remarkable that the same presuppositions are secretly at work in the philosophies that have claimed to reject the concepts of consciousness and subjectivity (or, in the case of ancient thought, those that did not even use these concepts). To know is always to see; to see is to see what is seen; what is seen is what stands there in front of us, what is put before us; it is the object. It exists to the extent that it is placed out in front, that it is object, that it is seen and known. Consciousness is this putting-forward as such, and knowledge is objectivity. The setting aside of the concepts of "subjectivity" and "consciousness" by post-Husserlian, Heideggerian, and post-Heideggerian phenomenology is really the rejection of everything that cannot be reduced to this primitive opening of the Outside in which the Object stands.

We have said that the distinctive feature of scientific knowledge is its objectivity. By that, we mean its supra-subjective and supra-individual character, its universality. What is true scientifically is such that it can be recognized by every mind (provided that it has the requisite competence). But the objectivity of scientific knowledge in its universality depends on the ontological objectivity that was just in question, in other words, on the fact that what is true must be able to be demonstrated. It ultimately must be able to be shown and brought into the condition of being there in front. It is in this condition of the object that every regard will be able to discover and see it in order to be assured of what it sees. Scientific knowledge is thus homogenous with the knowledge of consciousness in general and simply extends it, because it too obeys the *telos* of evidence. That is to say that they share the same effort to bring into full light before the regard that which will be clearly perceived in this light, and in this way, will be indubitable.[4]

The problem of culture – like the correlative problem of barbarism – can only become philosophically intelligible if it is deliberately referred to *a dimension of being where the knowledge of consciousness and of science (which is a developed form of consciousness) no longer intervene,* and if it is placed into relation with life and with life alone. That is the first implication of the claim that culture is the culture of life. It does not just signify that culture is the self-transformation of life. This self-transformation alone could only be blind. Inasmuch as it seeks growth, it must rely on a type of knowledge: *culture thus relies on another type of knowledge than that of science and consciousness.* This is the knowledge of life, and as we have indicated, life constitutes this knowledge by its own essence. It is the very fact of experiencing oneself in each point of one's being and thus this auto-revelation with which life begins and ends. What exactly does this original knowledge of life that is the basis of culture consist of? How does it differ from the knowledge of consciousness and science, to the point of excluding them irreparably from itself?

Let us consider a biology student who is reading a work about the genetic code. The student's reading is the repetition through an act of her own consciousness of the complex processes of conceptualization and theorizing contained in the book, or those that are signified by the printed characters. But, in order for this reading to be possible, the student must turn the pages with her hands as she reads. The student must move her eyes in order to cover it and collect the lines of the text one after the other. When the student becomes tired from her effort, she will get up, leave the library, and take the stairs to the cafeteria where she will get some rest and something to eat and drink. The knowledge contained in the biology manual that was assimilated by the student during her reading is scientific knowledge. The reading of the book uses a knowledge of consciousness; it consists partly in the perception of words, that is to say, in the sensible intuition of marks written on paper, and partly in the intellectual grasp of the ideal meanings that the words carry. Together, these meanings form the sense of the book, that is, the scientific knowledge contained in it. The knowledge that made possible the movements of the hands and the eyes, the act of getting up, climbing the stairs, drinking and eating, and resting is the knowledge of life.

If one were to ask which of these three types of knowledge is fundamental, it would be necessary to reject the prejudices of our time all at once: the beliefs that scientific knowledge is not only the most important but in reality the only true knowledge; that knowledge means science, that is, the type of mathematical knowledge of nature introduced at the time of Galileo; that everything prior to this arrival of rigorous science in the West was only a mass of disordered knowledge and confused feelings, if not prejudices and illusions. One should not forget, however, that beginnings are always what is the most difficult. How was prescientific humanity, lacking all of the tools that modern technology would later provide, able to survive and develop? Moreover, how was it ever able to produce extraordinary results in many domains, for example those of art and religion, that people of our time would be unable to achieve, unless it made use of this fundamental knowledge of life?

Let us look again at our biology student: *it is not scientific knowledge that allows her to acquire the scientific knowledge contained in the book.* It is not in virtue of this knowledge that she moves her hands or eyes or focuses her thoughts. Scientific knowledge is abstract; it is the intellectual intuition of a number of ideal meanings. But the act of moving the hands is not abstract at all. Scientific knowledge is objective, in this sense that it is the knowledge of an objectivity. An object can only be perceived, if it is in this condition of being-there in front and thus shows itself in this way and thus can be reached by a regard and thus can be known. *But knowing how to move the hands, knowing how to turn the eyes – this knowledge of life is not objective in any way or in any sense; it does not have an object because it does not contain in itself the relation to the object and because this relation is not its essence.*

If the knowledge contained in the movement of rubbing the hands and making it possible had an object, such as these hands and their potential movement, this movement would not happen at all. Knowledge would stand in front of it like it stands in front of something objective. It would be forever separated from it by the distance of objectivity, and it would be unable to ever rejoin it. To the extent that the movement of the hands is considered as something objective, and as long as it is considered this way, the possibility of acting on it and initiating it will seem enigmatic and magical for the one who considers it as an object. This enigma can vanish only by entering into life and by finding in it the essence that excludes every exteriority from it, because it excludes every relation to the object, every intentionality, and every ek-stasis from itself. Life alone has the ability to unite with the power of the hands and to identify with them, to be what it is and to do what it does. It alone possesses *a knowledge that merges with this power because it is nothing other than its continual experience of itself – its radical subjectivity.* It is only in and through the immanence of its radical subjectivity that the power of the hands, or of any power whatsoever, is possible. That is to say that it is in possession of itself and thus *can* be deployed at any moment. The knowledge of life is this knowledge that excludes the ek-stasis of objectivity from itself; it is a knowledge that sees nothing and for which there is nothing to see. Instead, it consists of the immanent subjectivity of its pure experience of itself and the pathos of this experience.

The knowledge of life (an expression that now seems tautological) is not only the external condition of scientific knowledge, in the sense that the scientist must know how to turn the pages of her book; it is also the internal condition of it. Scientific knowledge, as said above, is only a modality of the knowledge of consciousness, that is, of the relation to the object. But this too is only possible on the basis of the life within it. The relation to the object is the seeing of the object, whether it is the sensible seeing of the sensible object or the intellectual seeing of an intelligible object such as a number, an abstract relation, an ideality of some sort, etc. For the knowledge contained in the seeing of the object is not in any way exhausted by the knowledge of the object. It implies the knowledge of seeing itself. This knowledge is no longer consciousness, the intentional relation to the object, instead it is life.

This is what follows from Descartes's *cogito*, which is one of the most famous analyses in philosophical thought. In spite of the overabundance of commentaries on it, it usually remains misunderstood nonetheless. The main reason for this misinterpretation is interesting because it offers a remarkable example of what can be called the illusion of theoretical knowledge. This illusion takes on its most extreme form in modern culture where the referential content of discourse and the mode in which this content is presented and advanced on its own in the appearing of being is replaced by this discourse itself, that is to say, a text and its objective mode of givenness. The *cogito* is introduced in a text, the text of the first two Meditations. One can consider it as a part of this text, as a proposition, "I think therefore I am." That much is obvious. I understand well that in order to think I must exist. Likewise, I see that two plus three equals five, etc. What is evident is what consciousness sees in a clear and distinct seeing. It is the object of this seeing, in this case my existence that is implied by my thought. The *cogito*, presented and understood in this way, is a moment of theoretical knowledge, the first moment. It is also the model of all possible theoretical knowledge. Provided that it submits to this condition of clear and distinct seeing, it too will be certain and assured. As for this realization of theoretical knowledge in evidence, it is a modality of conscious knowledge in general, that is, a consciousness of objects.

If the text of the *cogito* is a proof within theoretical knowledge, what it means is something quite different. It is the putting out of play and exclusion of all knowledge of this kind – the knowledge of science and consciousness in general – in favor of another kind of knowledge whose essential and distinctive trait is to exclude every relation to the object and all objectivity from itself, and thus all evidence, including all theoretical or scientific knowledge. And this is how it happens.

Descartes calls into question seeing in general as the source and foundation of all knowledge whatsoever, whether it involves the sensible intuition of the sensible world or the intellectual intuition of rational truths. If the sensible world perhaps does not exist (if it is only a dream), if all of the rational truths are false (if the evil genius tricks me when I believe that two plus three equals five or that "in order to think, I must indeed exist"), it is only because seeing, all conceivable seeing, is fallacious, the clearest as well as the most confused. The evidence that seems the most indubitable – for example, that of the *cogito* – could not escape from a doubt that strikes evidence as such. But if seeing is in itself fallacious, if the place where everything becomes visible is not a place of visibility, it is not a making appear or a showing but an induction into error, a dissimulation and a mistake. If the transcendental condition of all possible knowledge is in itself, in reality, a principle of falsehood and error, how can any theoretical discourse whatsoever be carried out and how can human life even continue?

This can happen because it makes use of another type of knowledge from that which goes adrift in the First Meditation. This second knowledge is life, its feeling-oneself and experiencing-oneself-at-each-point-of-one's-being. This "feeling" and "experiencing" have no relation to objects or an object, no ek-stasis of a world or world. They are totally indifferent to the fate of this relation to the world and to the world itself, for example, with regard to its existence or nonexistence. So, when I dream, it might be the case that the room that I think I see and the persons to whom I believe I am speaking do not exist. But, if in the course of this dream, I experience a fright, this is what it is. It is absolutely, untouched and unaltered in its being by the fact that it is a dream and that there is no room or person or world. Its being remains untouched and unaltered by the alteration of seeing, by the disturbance of the ek-static site of visibility in which everything that is given for me to see becomes visible. If, in spite of the perversion of the relation to the world and the collapse of all objectivity, the fright remains intact, it means that the intentional relation to a world no longer enters into the fright and does not have any place in it. It means that the fright is never given through the intermediary of this relation, though any seeing whatsoever or the ek-stasis in which all seeing is based. How is fright given to itself? Inasmuch as it feels and experiences itself at each point of its being, in feeling-oneself as such which constitutes the essence of affectivity. Transcendental affectivity is the original mode of revelation in virtue of which life is revealed to itself and is thus possible as what it is, as life.

The knowledge of life is radically opposed to the knowledge of consciousness and science, to what we generally call knowledge. In the *cogitatio* – in the sense that most of the commentators on Descartes understand it, including Husserl and Heidegger – there is a *cogitatum*; consciousness is always conscious of something. It reveals something other than itself. With sensation, for example, something is sensed; it is revealed in and through this sensation. Likewise, perception reveals the perceived object, imagination an imaginary content, memory a remembrance, the understanding a concept, etc. In its own way of knowing, to the contrary, life does not reveal anything else: no alterity, no objectivity, nothing different from itself, nothing foreign to itself. And that is why it is life. What it originally senses is itself; what it originally experiences is itself, that by which it is originally affected is itself. Everything whose essence is to be auto-affected in the sense of being both what is affected and what affects – that and that alone is alive. But auto-affection is not an empty or formal concept, a speculative proposition. It defines the phenomenological reality of life itself – a reality whose substantiality is its pure phenomenality and whose pure phenomenality is transcendental affectivity. It is because the fright is nothing but the affectivity of its auto-affection that it *is* absolutely and could be nothing less, even if there were nothing but it in the world or even if there were no world. There would exist, in any case, this pure, mute experience of oneself that fright makes on its own, its passion – there would be life.

The being of fright remains intact, in the flesh of its affectivity, even though the representations that accompany it in the dream world reveal themselves to be illusory. What is true about fright is no less true for seeing itself, if we were to abstract from it everything that it sees and from seeing as a power of relating to what is seen and lets things be seen. For if this power to show were in reality a dissimulation, a deformation, and an induction into error, it would nonetheless exist in the pure experiencing of itself at each point of its being, as a living seeing. "*Sentimus nos videre*," says Descartes.[5] There is thus a feeling of oneself that remains in seeing and that is absolutely "true," even when the sight of this seeing and everything that it sees are both false.

One can see the condition for this. The subjective experience of seeing can only be absolutely "true" when seeing and what it sees are both false, if the power of revelation that reveals seeing itself is completely different from the power of revelation in which seeing discovers what is seen. The latter power is dubious. The power of revelation in which seeing is revealed to itself is the knowledge of life, that is to say, life itself. The power of revelation in which seeing discovers its object – what it sees – is the knowledge of consciousness. That is where science and all knowledge in general are based. These two powers are completely different from one another, because the latter is exhausted in the relation to the object and what ultimately founds it: the emergence of a first separation, the putting at a distance of a horizon, an ek-stasis. The phenomenality that initiates this is the power of transcendental exteriority in which every form of exteriority and objectivity are rooted, namely, the objectivity of science. In life's power of revelation, to the contrary, there is no longer any separation or distance. Life is an experience of oneself without distance. The phenomenality of this experience is affectivity.

Descartes never doubted the truth of science, even less did he want to be critical of it. Instead, his purpose is to justify science, quite precisely the very new mathematical science of nature that he discovers with wonder and in which he perceives extraordinary advances. But the genius of Descartes was to sense that this knowledge is not self-sufficient and that it presupposes another one, of another kind. Doubt, in the First Mediation, strikes every form of knowledge, whether sensible or intelligible, every relation to the object and thus every possible world, whatever it may be. By barring this relation and every form of knowledge recognized until then, the goal is to allow the secret knowledge that it harbors to appear. Descartes does not just affirm that there are two heterogeneous forms of knowledge, which he calls the knowledge of the soul or the ideas of the mind, on the one hand, and the knowledge of bodies or the relation to the object, on the other hand. The explicit theme of the Second Mediation is to show: 1) that the knowledge of the mind is more fundamental and more certain than the knowledge of the body – the title of the Meditation is "On the nature of the human mind and that it is more easily known than the body"; 2) that this absolutely certain knowledge of life is the basis for the knowledge of the body, that is to say, of the world, consciousness, and science in general.

The first proof is made by radically distinguishing the idea of the mind (or, the knowledge of the soul) from all other ideas that are the ideas of objects, whether real or ideal.[6] The difference is that the idea of the mind does not have a *cogitatum*, that is, it does not have an object. The idea of the mind is the original power of revelation in virtue of which the *cogitatio* (the soul or life) is the revelation of itself and not of any objectivity whatsoever as a *cogitatum*. So, fright reveals itself and does not reveal, in its affectivity, anything other than itself. The knowledge of life now (the knowledge of the soul) founds the knowledge of the body and all knowledge of objects. This results from the fact that the idea of the mind is not merely opposed to all other ideas; it constitutes their common essence. Each idea that has a *cogitatum* in it (the idea of a human, a triangle, or a God) can only come into being, if it is an idea of the mind and if, as an idea of the mind, it is first of all the pure and simple experience of oneself that reveals itself to itself as it is in itself, as a *cogitatio*, as a modality of life or the soul – even if there were no humans, triangles or God.

The seeing of an object presupposes the knowledge of seeing itself, and this knowledge of seeing is its own pathos. It is the auto-affection of absolute subjectivity in its transcendental affectivity (transcendental – what makes something possible as subjectivity and as life). To that extent, this seeing of an object is never merely a seeing. Because it constantly auto-affects and only sees through this auto-affection of itself, it is a sensibility. That is why the world is not a pure spectacle offered to an impersonal and empty gaze. It is a sensible world, not a world of consciousness but a *lifeworld*. That is to say that it is a world only given to life, which exists for life, in and through life. Every possible "world" is formed by the opening of an Outside, the originality Exteriorization of any exteriority whatsoever (for example, that of a number), but this production can only occur inasmuch as it affects itself, in and through the Affectivity of this production. This is why things are not sensible after the fact. They do not take on the tonalities with which they emerge before us as either threatening or serene, sad or indifferent, in virtue of the relations that they would establish through a history with our desires and with the endless play of our own interests. Instead, they do this and are able to do this, because they are affective from their birth and because there is a pathos of their coming into being as the coming of being to itself in the exaltation and suffering of life.

The abstraction made by science is thus twofold. First, it is abstraction that defines the scientific world as such. Sensible qualities and the affective predicates that belong to them *a priori* are put out of play from the being of nature so that they only retain the forms capable of giving them an ideal determination. This nonconsideration of the subjective features of every possible world is indispensable from a methodological point of view, inasmuch as it allows for the establishment of procedures such as quantitative measurement that permit types of knowledge to be obtained that otherwise would be inaccessible. But, the infinite development of this ideal knowledge can only be pursued legitimately inasmuch as it remains clearly conscious of the limits of its field of investigation, limits that it has drawn itself. It cannot escape the fact that the setting aside of the sensible and affective properties of the world presupposes the setting aside of life itself, that is to say, of what makes up the humanity of the human being. That is the second abstraction made by science in the current sense: the abstraction of Life and of what alone truly matters.

Yet, the term "abstraction" is quite weak here and no longer entirely appropriate. If science does indeed perform an "abstraction" of the sensible predicates of nature by no longer taking them into consideration in its methodologies and calculations, it nonetheless develops on the basis of this nature of which it retains only the traits that matter to it. It is indeed the knowledge of these traits that it ultimately seeks by following its chosen paths. *Science, to the contrary, has no idea of what life is; it is in no way concerned with it; it has no relation to it and never will.* There can only be access to life in and through life, if it is the case that only life is related to itself in the Affectivity of its auto-affection. In life's "relation to itself," there is no "relation to," no ek-stasis, no "consciousness," but science operates entirely and exclusively in the relation to the world. It only knows the world and its objects. It is objective, due to its ultimate ontological foundations. That is why it does not know and will never know that which experiences itself and auto-affects itself in and only in the radical immanence of its affectivity. It will never know what presents itself and essentializes itself in oneself as life.

The world is a pure site of exteriority. Everything that is conditioned by the world can only ever be offered as an exterior-being. It can only be a section of exteriority, a surface, a region offered to a regard. This regard slides along forever without ever being able to penetrate the interior of what is concealed from it behind a new aspect, a new façade or a new screen. For this exterior being does not have an interior. Its law is becoming, the continual emergence of new sides and new planes. Knowledge pursues the succession of all these lures. Each one is presented to it, only then to immediately conjure away a being that it does not have and to refer to the next one. This new lure plays the same game in turn. No interior: nothing is alive *that can speak in its own name, in the name of what it experiences,* in the name of what it is. They are only "things," only death. The advance of the world and its ek-static disclosure can only display and ex-pose what is always in front and outside: the object.

By putting out of play not only the lifeworld but, more seriously, life itself or what we are, the play of knowledge is laden with significant consequences from the outset. If the auto-transformation and growth of culture is the business of life, what we have only glimpsed now appears with a striking clarity: since science has no relation with culture, the development of science has nothing to do with the development of culture. At the limit, one can imagine an extreme development of scientific knowledge that would go along with an atrophy of culture, with its regression in some domains or in all domains at once and, at the end of this process, its annihilation. This image is neither ideal nor abstract. It is the actual world we live in, a world which has just given rise to a new type of barbarism that is more serious than any that have preceded it and from which human beings risk dying from today.

I call "praxis" the knowledge of life, as a knowledge in which life is at once the power that knows and what is known by it. Life provides the sole "content" of this knowledge. What characterizes this kind of knowledge, as we have seen, is that all ek-stasis is absent from it and there is no relation to any "world" whatsoever in it. By contrast, I call "theory" the knowledge that defines this relation to the world. Theory is the theory of an object. Still, with respect to everything, we speak about a practical point of view and a theoretical point of view and their difference, as something that is self-evident. The principle behind this difference, however, remains obscure, and that is because it is rooted in the ultimate structures of Being and ultimately in its invisible Basis. It is only there that it can be elucidated.

Inasmuch as culture is the culture of life and rests on this type of knowing, it is essentially practical. It consists of the self-development of the subjective potentialities of life. Take the case of seeing, which our analysis has taken as an example to help us understand the nature of this original knowledge of life. Everyone will easily distinguish between the vulgar eye, which Marx speaks about in his *1844 Manuscripts*, that is unable either to form a distinct perception of what it considers or to have an artistic appreciation of it and the cultivated eye whose refined exercise is, in its pathos, aesthetic pleasure. As for subjective motor potentialities, everyone will similarly be able to distinguish between the body of a dancer, which is able to master its force and, it seems, increase it, and the body of an untrained and awkward person. Similar distinctions can be made for the diction of an actor, the breathing of a singer, etc. We can now say more about the knowledge of life and understand why culture is not simply the use of powers that are defined once and for all but in fact their "development."

As a practice, culture adopts different forms. First of all, its elementary forms are the concrete modalities for the fulfillment of immediate living. Thus each culture is characterized by specific ways of actively producing the goods that are useful to life and consuming them. This includes food, clothing, shelter, etc., as well as the spontaneous play of life, such as the celebration of its destiny, eroticism, the relation to death. This conduct gets expressed in various rituals that give each society its own physiognomy. The social organization with its seemingly objective structure is only the external representation in the theoretical seeing of what is actually a praxis. Its reality is found in and only in the life of absolute subjectivity. There it finds the principle of its development and the "laws" that govern it. *These laws are not the laws of consciousness; they are not theoretical laws joined to the way that we represent things and think; they are practical laws, laws of life.* As such, they originate from subjectivity. They are presented and act as needs, in the sense that we will give to this word. These needs will be understood on the basis of the essence of life, as prescribed and sought by this essence. Need and work are thus two elementary modalities of praxis situated in the extension of the one by the other. Work or rather spontaneous activity is nothing other than the outgrowth of need and its fulfillment.

Yet, subjectivity is entirely need. Higher needs, which result from the nature of need, give rise to the developed forms of culture: art, ethics, and religion. The presence of these "higher" forms in each known civilization is not merely an empirical fact to be acknowledged. Instead, art, ethics, and religion are rooted in the essence of life. The reason for their emergence becomes intelligible to anyone who understands this essence.

Likewise, barbarism – which is the regression of the modes of fulfillment of life and the end put to fulfillment – is not an incomprehensible and disastrous event that strikes a culture from the outside at the height of its bloom. Its successive contamination of every domain of social activity, the gradual disappearance, in the organic totality of a human "world," of its aesthetic, ethical and religious dimensions, can also be understood. It is a process that affects the essence of being, understood as the principle from which all culture and all of it concrete modalities of realization, including the highest ones, proceed. It is a sickness of life itself.

Our questions – concerning barbarism in its historical provenance from culture as well as culture itself as the prerequisite of this whole development – are organized as follows:

1. How should we understand the very possibility of culture and ultimately the essence of life? What must life be in order to make the development of a culture possible *a priori* and thus necessary?

2. How does this development take place in order to end up with "higher" forms? Why do these forms take on the specific, concrete modalities of art, ethics and religion?

3. If life necessarily produces culture and its movement of self-transformation strives for self-growth, how is it possible for this movement to invert into the processes of decay and impoverishment? It is not barbarism itself that is strange, if one really thinks about it. It is its possibility, its provenance from an essence that is constructed internally as self-growth and that implies culture. One would have to confuse the absolute phenomenological life with biological life and naïvely understand the former on the basis of the latter, in order for phenomena of decay which bother living organisms to be transferred onto the level of social edifices and in order for the decline and collapse of these edifices to appear "natural." Civilizations are mortal, like individuals, that's all.

Like biological individuals! The individuals in question in the sphere of culture or barbarism really have nothing to do with the collections of molecules whose scattering can be observed at the end of an objective process. Because they are modes of absolute life and carry its essence of self-growth within themselves, the thought of their disappearance or their decay is not merely experienced by them as a scandal. In the eyes of the philosopher who can enter into the essence of living beings, it is discovered to be an *a priori* impossibility. Nietzsche's genius was to have perceived this *aporia* and to have gone to extraordinary lengths in order to solve it.

Down here everything rises and falls. The view from above over all of external-being internalizes what it has learned about things and then tries to adjust to it as best it can. This is what one calls wisdom – the wisdom of historians, sociologists, ethnologists, and biologists, and all those who trust in what they see. But one does not yet know anything about life when one "philosophizes" in this way. Life is discovered as an unauthorized (*sauvage*) principle within oneself that has to do with a knowledge that one does not have. To the extent that one can know what it is, it obeys different laws from those that one seeks to teach the philosopher in the treatises of the positive sciences. It does not contrast with them through vague ambitions and dreams but through reality, pure and simple. This reality produces couples and societies and never ceases to produce them. It propels them toward their own culture, which is the culture of Desire. Desire is not modeled on things because it is the Desire of Life and thus the Desire of the Self.

The question that we are raising in this book cannot do without the questions that have been stated above. To understand the decadence of our times requires us to understand how the decline of Life in general is possible. But the task is still more precise. It is a matter of demonstrating the specific character of the barbarism to come, and we are already stumbling around blindly in its shadow. The claim that the disarray of the present time results from the extreme development of scientific knowledge and the technologies to which it has given rise and from its rejection of the knowledge of life will surely seem too general and excessive. It is thus important to prove it through the use of precise examples. Art will be evoked first, and this example is not by chance. It will serve to reveal what provisionally will be called "the barbarism of science."

Notes

1   See Husserl, *The Crisis of the European Sciences and Transcendental Philosophy,* trans. David Carr (Evanston: Northwestern University Press, 1970).

2   Unpublished manuscript by Edmund Husserl (May 1934).

3   John B. Watson, *The Ways of Behaviorism* (New York: Harpers, 1928), 7.

4   The change of the conditions of objectivity in modern science and in particular to the microphysical scale does not change anything about the ultimate requirement of a givenness in presence, without which no experimentation or theorizing would be possible.

5   René Descartes, "Lettre à Plempius," in *Oeuvres I,* eds. Charles Adam and Paul Tannery (Paris: Vrin, 1983), 413.

6   Descartes, "Réponses aux sixièmes objections," in *Oeuvres VII,* 443.

2 SCIENCE JUDGED BY THE CRITERION OF ART

Science as such has no relation with culture, because it develops outside of its realm. We sought to establish this situation in the preceding chapter, and on its own it does not justify any pejorative evaluation or condemnation that would lead to the disqualification of science. The philosopher has the duty to intervene only when the domain of science is understood as the sole existing domain of true being and subsequently leads to the rejection of the domain of life and culture into nonbeing or an illusory appearance. Once again, it is not scientific knowledge that is in question; it is the ideology joined to it today which holds that it is the sole possible knowledge and that all other ones must be eliminated. Amidst the collapse of all beliefs, that is the sole belief that persists in the modern world, the previously encountered and universally echoed conviction that knowledge means science.

If we take the criterion of art in order to evaluate the relation of science to culture, we become disoriented. We find ourselves truly faced with nothingness. *Art is an activity of sensibility, the fulfillment of its powers, whereas modern science, with the elimination of sensible qualities from nature, defines its own field and defines itself through the exclusion of this sensibility.* Science and art thus fall outside of one another. The heterogeneity between their respective domains is so radical that the very thought of a relation between the two is, at least for the moment, impossible.

One need not bother with the superficial objection that it would be possible to find many "beauties" in scientific work and its products. The photographic pictures acquired with the help of microscopes of various powers are rightly famous not only for the strangeness of the world that they allow us to perceive but also, and this is what interests us here, for the harmony of the representations that they bring us. Along with their power to captivate us, this harmony gives them an undeniable aesthetic character. Thus, one should not be surprised to see these photographs in many works of art, set alongside, for instance, pictorial works that are called "avant-garde" and are used to justify it. Besides, many artists, including some of the greatest, have sought to give their art a cognitive meaning. They have sought to go to the heart of things and to provide a new revelation of them. Here it suffices to cite names such as Leonardo da Vinci and Albrecht Dürer.

More recently, the surprising parallel that has been established between some plastic investigations and a number of scientific discoveries, for example, of microscopic phenomena. This is an indication, if not a proof, of the unity of knowledge as well as its universality. Each truly original and thus unusual production in the domain of graphic or pictorial creation can put forward the case for its unforeseen but undeniable resemblance with some document brought to light by fundamental research and receive some type of validation from it. Kandinsky was thus overwhelmed by becoming aware of Bohr's theories about the atom. He saw in them a dissolution of objective reality or at least a deconstruction of what was taken to be the nature of things until then. He thereby found a powerful motif that gave full development to some of his intuitions. This resulted in what would come to be called "abstract painting."

For the present time, let us limit ourselves to observing that the rapprochement between certain aesthetic works, on the one hand, and scientific works, on the other hand, has the opposite meaning from the one that we imagined we could give to it. The fact that the veins of a leaf or the structures of a crystal resemble the results of exercises practiced on pure graphic elements like the point, line, etc., or the fact that photographs from the microscope or plant or mineral forms might support a comparison with pictorial works, even the most innovative ones, does not show that the domain of science overlaps, even partially, with the domain of art, that is, with sensibility and life. Quite the contrary, it is not as "scientific" and as revealing a scientific truth, as documents for the validation or refutation of pure theories that these reproductions of crystal, plant, or other structures have an aesthetic value. It is inasmuch as they are given to human sensibility. For this reason and it alone can a certain construction or layout of elements have a plastic meaning. *The laws that make these scientific documents beautiful are the aesthetic laws of sensibility; they are not the mathematical or physical laws that the scientist seeks to decipher in them.*

If such representations, apart from their meaning for the scientist, offer another meaning to the artist or the lover of art, it is precisely because the scientific world is abstract and because it is derived from the nonconsideration of the sensible elements that belong *a priori* to nature and all natural things. Colors and sensible forms remain on the photographic plates where they are able to move us through the harmony of their presentation. This shows that they cannot be eliminated from nature and that Galilean abstraction consists only in not paying them any attention. It no longer lets them enter into its calculations, but it never suppresses them. This is because colors and forms are constitutive of the being of nature. Real nature is sensible nature and not the world of idealities that science substitutes for it in its constructions and theories. Scientific data and science itself are thus only able to be "beautiful" inasmuch as, beyond and even through their abstraction, they ultimately refer to the sole world that exists – the lifeworld.

Why does art necessarily emerge in the human experience as one of the fundamental forms of all culture? That is one of our questions, and we are already able to provide some answer to it. Nature is essentially a sensible nature, because the relation to the object and ultimately the ek-stasis of being where all nature and this relation itself are based, is auto-affective in its own transcendence, such that seeing, for example, is a sensible seeing. That is why Kant, who sought the conditions of all possible experience, or in his terms, of every possible world, began his investigation with a Transcendental Aesthetic – with the analysis of sensibility. Without a doubt, this analysis unfolds on a plane that is still the plane of factuality. It *encounters* sensibility at the birth of the world, without truly understanding the reason for the sensible character of this birth. But this reason is available to us: the world is a sensible world because it is a lifeworld and not a pure consciousness. It is affective in its basis, according to the innermost possibility of its ek-static display.

Sensibility not only is the *a priori* essence of every possible world but also defines the possibility of art. "It is only through sensibility that one can reach the truth in art," declares Kandinsky. And he adds: "Art acting on sensibility, it can also only act through sensibility." This is how the famous laws of beauty, as laws of sensibility, only appear to be mathematical, ideal, and objective laws. Even when one would be able to give forms, the relations between them, and the various plastic elements of a composition, a rigorous mathematical formulation, this would only ever be the ideal approximation of proportion and balance that are at play in sensibility. They find their possibility, the demands to which they respond, and their ultimate reason in sensibility. That is why, as Kandinsky says, "Balance and proportion cannot be found outside of the artist but within him."[1]

To the degree that it employs the powers of sensibility, art does not constitute a separate domain. It enters into harmony with the world and every possible world in general, if it is the case that the world is a sensible world that is born in sensibility and sustained by it. The lifeworld – which is the real world in which humans live – thus falls entirely under the categories of the aesthetic and is only comprehensible through them. It is a world that is necessarily either beautiful or ugly. And, if it is neither one, it is a sort of average neutrality that is one aesthetic determination among others. It is in some state of the sensibility to which this world is devoted in principle. Every culture includes art as one of its essential features, because this belongs naturally to the lifeworld in which humans live. Every human being living in this world is potentially an artist, at any rate those for whom sensibility functions as the transcendental condition of this world and its emergence.

What now must be understood is the meaning of this putting out of play of sensibility by science and its exclusion from the world for which it is the founding possibility. *Stricto sensu*, this exclusion is impossible since, as we just noted, sensibility is the transcendental condition of everything that can take the form of a "world." Sensibility is only eliminated from the scientific world. And that is the reason why the scientific world is abstract. This means that it is a world in which sensibility is no longer taken into account, even though it remains there as its unperceived condition. This is what the study of photographic reproductions of various materials in the microscope just showed. Their scientific character did not prevent them from appearing, inasmuch as this was an appearance of a world with "aesthetic" qualities.

The situation is thus in reality as follows. There is only one world, and it is the lifeworld. It is possible to act toward this world in such a way that one puts its sensible qualities out of play and is no longer concerned with them at all. In this way, one introduces changes into the world that have their premises in and only in the ideal determinations of science. One is then in the presence of *effects produced in a world that is necessarily a world of sensibility but sensibility itself is no longer considered*. This sensibility does not disappear. The sensible elements remain as inescapable supports of this lifeworld. It just happens that these sensible features are no longer determined and arranged in terms of the inner laws of sensibility: *an essentially aesthetic world will cease to obey aesthetic prescriptions*. That is the barbarism of science, and here are some examples of it.

In Greece, at Eleusis, there are remains of one of the fortresses that protected Attica in the sixth century. It is an impressive wall with enormous blocks of stone shining in the sun – above them, unfortunately, there is a high voltage line. It serves to transport electrical current from one place to another. In calculating the best conditions for this operation, the solution adopted by Greek engineers was probably the good one. If it provides us with one of the countless examples of the barbarism that ravages our world, this is because these calculations become possible by abstracting from sensibility. We understand a little better what sensibility is and what its nonconsideration by science means. Sensibility does not delineate a particular domain of human experience; it is not a region of Being that could be neglected in order to better devote oneself to another one. As its substrate, sensibility is the Whole of experience and thus the Whole of the world; the world is necessarily offered as a Whole in sensibility. It is a huge illusion to believe that there is something like an objective totality and that the world is like a huge sack containing everything, where beings and things can be placed side by side: stone, earth, sky, electrical currents, and human beings. No world can be a pure world; no radical exteriority can be reduced to it alone. In a site of radical exteriority, each element would be so foreign to all the others that it would not be able to enter into any relation with them, not even exteriority. As a result, such a site is not even conceivable. When we speak about the world as a site of pure exteriority, in reality we are presupposing something else. We are presupposing the unity of this site, that is to say, this "site" as such – in this case, the auto-affection of the ek-stasis of exteriority which, in and through this auto-affection, makes it possible as exteriority.

What we have just described is the sensible world, a world whose unity and possibility is sensibility. In sensibility, everything is connected as One and is held in a Unity; it is thus in relation with everything else that exists. This is the reason why it is not possible, with regard to sensibility, to only consider one thing and to neglect all of the others. Like the Greek engineers, one might be interested only in the electrical current and in the means of transporting it, in the calculations concerning it and what they require, such as the height of the poles, the resistance of the wires, the frequency of the current, etc. All of these "elements" nonetheless belong to one single world, the one in which the fortress stands. It is not situated under the line in virtue of a mere external relation, such as the spatial relation of the one-outside-of-the-other, the one-next-to-the-other, or the one-under-the-other. The fortress in itself is no more "under" the electrical line than the line passes "over" it. In an external and purely spatial relation constituted by the exteriority of space, they have no relation to one another. They are neither near nor far. If, after some kind of cataclysm such as an earthquake, a broken cable were to fall onto the stone wall and rest on one of the stones, it would not "touch" it. Even the image of millions of light years would be a weak representation, or rather wholly inadequate, to convey an idea of the infinitely infinite distance that would forever separate them.

The fortress and the electrical line can only be arranged one next to the other or one "below" the other within the unity of sensibility. As an auto-affection of the ek-stasis of exteriority, sensibility is essentially individual, because auto-affection as such constitutes the essence of every possible ipseity. The individual is thus the Whole of being, that in and through which what exists is always taken into a Whole and offered as such. It is because an Individual stands in front of them, not as an empirical individual in space but as the ipseity of all plurality and all ek-static division, that the fortress and line are together in the same world. The laws of their unified relation are the laws of sensibility, that is to say of this Joining (*Indivis*) by the Individual. They are aesthetic laws. What the nonconsideration of sensibility by science means has become altogether clear now: it is a putting together, in this case of the line and the fortress, without any consideration of the laws that ultimately underlie every possible putting together. These laws are not abolished, however, any more than the aesthetic world that is composed on the basis of them. It turns out that the aesthetic nature of the world receives its figure in the modern age: the horrible and horror.

The role of science becomes all the more precise when one seeks to enter inside of aesthetics, understood this time as a discipline of knowledge. The word "aesthetic" necessarily has many meanings. Conforming to the fundamental structures of being and their original division, it can be understood in two senses, practical and theoretical. As a praxis, aesthetics refers to a modality of the life of sensibility, and correlatively to its world, the lifeworld as a sensible world. The specific activity of the artist, or the art lover, is only an actualization of the life of sensibility, its use for and by itself, its self-development, its self-fulfillment, and thus its growth. *Stricto sensu*, the relation between the life of sensibility and the aesthetic life offers a privileged example of the general relation between life and culture and how the one is only the actualization of the other.

The term "aesthetic" can also refer to a theoretical discipline, and its object is the aesthetic reality that we just described. Clearly, this object is twofold. It is partly the sensibility of the world that belongs to it. Kant gave the name Transcendental Aesthetic to the study of sensibility thus understood. It is also partly the dimension of culture in which the life of sensibility arrives at its highest forms of actualization. One usually calls "aesthetics" the theoretical discipline that pursues the study of these higher forms of artistic creation and the brilliant works which result from it.

If every culture is essentially practical, the very possibility of a theoretical culture appears problematic and first presents itself as an aporia. How could invisible life – which has no figure or face, no inside or outside, no front or back, no profile or side, no surface, no external aspect, no face of its being turned toward an outside and offered to a regard – one day be attained, encountered, examined, and known by this regard? One might say that aesthetic activity as praxis, as a mode of sensibility and thus of life, remains unknown and immersed in the mysterious depths in which all creation is enveloped, especially artistic creation. This theoretical discipline of aesthetics, however, can provide an object – namely, the artwork itself – as the subject matter for its knowledge, which indisputably belongs to a world in its objectivity. We will show that the artwork is nothing of this sort, and that its supposed objectivity is only an appearance. Analysis must necessarily pass through it, if it wants to arrive at the place where the artwork really stands. The question of a theoretical culture, that is to say of a theorization of praxis, thus remains at the center of every reflection on culture, as one of its required themes. We will not tackle that question here. Our problem, for the present time, is narrower: provided that we have established the possibility of a theoretical aesthetic, we must measure the effect of the introduction of science into it. If aesthetics still has a legitimate role for human beings, does it too not depend on escaping the subjective impressions and contingent opinions of individuals? Does it not depend on being "scientific"?

Half way between Athens and Eleusis, on the ancient sacred route, there stands the Daphni monastery. On the site of an ancient sanctuary for Apollo, a Basilica was built in the fifth century in order to attract the pilgrims who went there for the last celebrations of Orphic cults to Christianity. Abandoned and in ruins during the "dark ages" of Attica, it was rebuilt in the year 1100 by an illustrious Christian, we are told, who decorated the new church "with splendid mosaics and polychromatic marbles." Mosaics are the most noble and rich of all expressive surfaces, but they are fragile. So it is a miracle that at the end of the eventful history of the monastery – which served as a refuge to Greek patriots during the revolution, a barracks, and an insane asylum – these mosaics were able to survive up to today. After being restored at the end of the century, today they are offered to people in their former splendor.

To restore is to reestablish the material integrity of an artwork or rather its physical support, to the extent that it has been damaged. The artwork in itself is nothing material. The tiles of a mosaic, the wood or copper of an engraving, the canvas of a painting, the colors that cover it are indeed "things" that belong to our surrounding world. But, in aesthetic experience (regardless of whether it is the experience of the creator or the spectator), these material elements only serve to depict a reality of another order, the reality represented by the painting, engraving or mosaic. That reality belongs to the artwork itself. One can perceive the canvas of the painting, examine its grain, its cracks, and this is something that is done when one seeks to date it with precision. In the case of a painting on wood, one will say that it is Flemish if it is made of oak or Italian if it is made of fir. Once aesthetic seeing begins and once the "canvas" or the "wood" becomes a "painting" and thereby enters into the true dimension of the work of art, however, it is "neutralized." It is no longer perceived or posited as an object of the world but as an entity whose sole function is to depict the reality represented in the painting. This reality, too, is neutralized and does not belong to the real world any more than the elements that represent it. Together they consti-tute a single, new dimension of being in which they are unified by relations of resemblance. This is the ontological dimension of art. In the aesthetic contemplation of the Dürer engraving "Knight, Death, and the Devil," to borrow the famous example used by Husserl, we are not directed toward the engraved plaque or the figurines appearing in dark lines on it but toward the "figurative realities" that are "portrayed" or "depicted."[2] They do not con-stitute the engraving as an object of the world but the engraved-object as an artwork, its aesthetic reality.

We are saying that an artwork is destroyed when its material support no longer exists or undergoes a serious alteration, such that the repetition of it – based on the perception of this support, of the aesthetic object itself, of the imaginary and spiritual work – can no longer happen. To restore is thus to reconstitute this substrate by putting its former components back into place or, when they have disappeared, through the construction or mount-ing of identical elements that will play an identical role. That is to say that, on the basis of them and as depicted by them, perception will redeploy the same "work" in the aesthetic dimension of the imaginary.

The restoration of artworks is imposed as a permanent task of civiliza-tion, because their material supports are changed by the effects of time, if not by natural catastrophes or the misdeeds of human beings: fires, earth-quakes, wars, voluntary degradation, etc. Every aesthetic work, it should be recalled, is offered as a totality and is only intelligible as such. In a picture each color takes on its value only in terms of all the other ones, whether they are contiguous to it or joined to it in a more subtle relation by a distant or opposed point on the canvas. The same goes for each form and each volume. Every element of what is thus called a composition is necessary to the appearance of the composition and "belongs" to it in this very pre-cise sense. *This composition is an aesthetic composition.* The relations out of which a composition is made, the elements out of which these relations are established, have an aesthetic nature. They are situated within the artwork's dimension of irreality. When the painter places a color on the canvas, it is not the color that is examined; the composition is seen. The painter sees what corresponds to this stroke or this patch – in short, its aesthetic effect. They are integrated into the collection of effects, which is to say, into the Whole of the artwork. So, in front of a Franz Hals, one must back up several steps to the place where these large brush strokes will change immediately into a rosy cheek, or on the face of the Officer of the Civil Guard of St. Adrian who turns slowly toward us, into the eye of Life that looks at us through time.

Aesthetic composition is certainly not this palette of colors that the canvas has become as a result of the artist's pencil or knife marks, but it is only possible on that basis. Each plastic element of the composition is formed out of a material element; it presupposes its existence. To the plastic whole of the composition, which is the work itself, there necessarily corresponds an organic unity of the substrate. To the particular resemblance that is established each time between a part of the canvas and its aesthetic equivalent, there corresponds an overall resemblance between the work and its support. This is offered as a continuum; it has a sort of unity. It is not an internal unity that only belongs to the work, since the material use of colors is determined by the aesthetic effect that it will produce. It is in order to produce this effect that this material use is necessary. It is the continuum presented by the material substrate of the work that makes it into the analogue, that on the basis of which it will be able to emerge and unfold in its own dimension of existence. And that is the reason why this continuum should be preserved at all costs or reestablished and reconstituted when it has been damaged or destroyed.

In the case of the Daphni monastery, the aesthetic unity of each one of the paintings that decorates its vaults and naves has added a higher unity that cannot be overlooked. The tiles – the little cubes of glass and cut stones – are used to depict and represent the content of the mosaic's aesthetic composition. But what do they represent? What is this content that is inadequately qualified by affirming its irreality? At Daphni, like many other of its contemporary or analogous structures, there is a collection of religious scenes that are said to "represent" the life of Christ as well as the adventures of persons who, in some way, have taken part in his life. In this way, we discover the higher unity which we have mentioned. All of the representations arranged on the interior walls of the church and on the exonarthex represent the same thing. To put it straightaway, they represent the original essence of life that produces every culture and out of which various cultural forms, in particular art, are developed. The representation of life is, in this case, a representation of Christ Almighty whose huge image is enthroned at the top of the large dome. Because life is understood here in its ultimate Basis as the Source and nurturing Principle of everything that is alive, it is quite precisely the procession of that natural forms of life – these forms of life do not engender themselves but experience a radical passivity with regard to the Basis that engenders them and continually does so – that is depicted on the walls of Daphni. Thus, around the Archi-Icon of the center and as manifestations or emanations of its Power that secretly depend on it, the people of sacred history are arranged: the Mother, the arch angels, the prophets, the martyrs, the saints, the ascetics. The events connected to the life of each one of them are related on levels, according to scales that are a function of their respective importance, that is to say, of the degree of their proximity or distance with regard to the Principle.

The Byzantine monastery thus offers a striking example of an altogether remarkable aesthetic composition. The law of its construction, that is to say the plastic arrangement of its elements, is like the reflection of a metaphysical composition that assigns each thing its place according to the degree of its ontological participation in the One. This metaphysical or mystical principle of aesthetic composition gives Byzantine art its tremendous force. Put alongside other types of composition, such as the Greek type that sought the spatial laws of constructing the being of things and evoked them in terms of the modalities of depth, perspective, etc., it would flatten them and reduce their attempt to spatial arrangements. If the various "renaissances" that mark the history of Byzantine art have not known the full blossoming of the last one of them, namely the Italian Renaissance, it is not due to a lack of know how or insufficient theoretical knowledge. This can be seen in Sopocani's paintings whose characters have the monumental stature of those of Piero and Michelangelo, who then add a spiritual force that is later lost. This is because the processional structure of the internal constitution of being always prevailed over its mere intuitive and spatial representation. The conception of this processional structure makes the religious edifice the microcosm of metaphysical reality and gives it a properly spiritual unity. This conception finds its aesthetic repetition in mural representations that, apart from their own aesthetic unity, appear as the various parts of one single and unique monumental composition. Whether one is a believer or not, the emotion of anyone who enters into the sanctuary blends with the vague perception of this plastic continuum that offers the mysterious image of what it is.

But, it is not this happy emotion but stupor that takes hold of the visitor to Daphni who, in the silence of the sanctuary, stands motionless at the entrance of the exonarthex. What is there no longer takes place like it did before, with marvelous gradations of light and colors that play with endless nuances, the continuity of a vessel with striking covering where the endless becoming of being out of its secret source is announced. They are all hidden by scaffoldings which lead the rare tourists who still go there to believe that this is a work of restoration. Huge white streaks of stucco and cement spread out their monstrous tentacles, sowing desolation and horror where they once shone with the scintillating tonalities of cut glass and colored stones. The sacred scenes are literally torn apart, forever deprived of sense and life. The circle around the Almighty, the heavenly lamb, is broken. The tiles of gold on the large dome have been detached and replaced by these empty surfaces that are everywhere, under the vaults, in the tubes, along the arches, on entire sections of the narthex walls, drawing their archipelago of death. Let there be no mistake: these squirts of cement that are scattered over the four corners, like dislocated limbs, the fragments of depositions, annunciations, and baptisms, are not provisional. It is the definitive state of places that are presented to us in the appalling appearance of this shattered meaning, of this plastic unity divided into fragments and pulverized.

What is happening? Due to its continual theoretical progress, today science has developed various comparative methods that allow us to date material in a rigorous way, and consequently, to distinguish in a restored work between what is original and what is not. The fact that these tiles do not belong to the original mosaic and that they only came about in 1890 to take the place of ones that had disappeared is an irrefutable, objective, scientific truth. The term "objective" can be taken in the dual sense established above. It is undeniable and must be recognized by everyone, because it is objective in a more radical, ontological sense. It can be posited and placed right in front of us, standing under the gaze. Everyone can see it and see it again in order to verify and note it as often as one wants: the notation of a laboratory formula. This hold that we have on reality, this way of controlling it, of being able to lay it bare in front of us and to display it as it is, to say whether it dates from the sixteenth, seventeenth, or nineteenth century, is not only our knowledge but an absolute knowledge. This is not to say that it is complete but that there is no other knowledge than it and no other science different from science. For that reason as well, this knowledge must guide our action. Our action does not differ from science, to the extent that our only relation to life is an intentional relation and thus the relation to objects, and thus to the extent that our only comportment toward being consists of bringing it into this condition which is and must be its own. It is there in front and displays itself there in order for its own being to be disclosed. The physico-mathematical approach determines what we truly perceive of being and seek from it, what we can expect of it, and what we can legitimately do with it. What matters in the Byzantine monastery is what stands before us; it is something that can be turned into something objective in this way and for this end; it is something that can be established scientifically, namely, the discrimination between various additions, touch ups, and other repainting made to the original work. The hammer marks of the demolition workers who systematically tear down these additions express very precisely what science has to say on the subject of the Daphni monastery; they are the rigorous consequence of its knowledge and its wishes.

For the first time in the history of art, we now have a very specific type of restoration. It does not redo what was undone. It does not patch up fallen tiles on the basis of preliminary sketches. It does not revive faded colors. It does not try to provide a possible repetition of the plastic living unity of the composition by reconstituting the material continuum of the support. It does just the opposite. It tears down and blindly removes what patient generations of admirers, artisans, and artists had done in order to give the masterpiece the fullness of its beauty and sense. That is a new form of barbarism. It is no longer based on ignorance and misery, on the pillage and coveting of precious objects, but on science, its organisms and funds.

One might object that science does not prescribe any goal to our actions and that, whatever its own approach toward being might be, it does not need to be accountable for our use of its increasingly different methods in which it expresses an increasingly developed knowledge. Does chemical analysis tell us to bury everything that does not date from the twelfth century? *But who will say this?* Shouldn't some other discipline other than physics be introduced here, one which takes into consideration the aesthetic aspect of the monastery – a discipline called "aesthetics"?

But will this aesthetics be scientific? Will it have the means, by setting aside every subjective impression and thus every discourse on and about the work of art, to provide evidence of a body of rigorous and positive knowledge? Will its project be to display what will be recognized and established with certainty in and through an explicit and objective mode of presentation? As a result, its object will be everything that comes to appear through a specific method and that responds to the demands of this method. It will be an element of the domain of science in question and at the same time the proof of its effectiveness and reality. It is precisely when aesthetics understood the need to behave toward the work of art as the other sciences do toward nature – to submit it to a method of investigation that ensures itself in universal, rational, and certain determinations – that it became scientific. As one sees at Daphni, it forced the monastery to deliver over its secrets and to confess, as a result of analysis, about what it truly is. Because anything that does not come into objectivity in the light of a scientific approach to it is nothing at all, it only needs to be pushed aside, along with the rubble and sweepings.

In order to take stock of what the exclusion of sensibility from the life-world means, we have chosen the criterion of art. This is what led us to our first, brief analysis of the aesthetic object, and it presents us with an aporia. On the one hand, we are saying that the artwork is constituted on the basis of its material support but goes beyond it. The work of art is imaginary. It develops outside of the real world and thus in a dimension of irreality. It is precisely the misunderstanding of the ontological status of the work of art by scientific knowledge and scientific aesthetics (that extends its objectivist aim) that leads such an "aesthetics" to confuse the artwork with its support. It imagines that the authenticity of the artwork overlaps rigorously with authenticity of the support, and if the support has been remade, the original work no longer exists. And that is what leads to the monstrous destruction about which we have spoken, and unfortunately Daphni offers only one example among many others of this.

On the other hand, we have stated that the world of sensibility is the real world of life and that the scientific world is only an abstraction of it. As such, the real world is a world of sensibility that draws its contents and laws from sensibility – it is an aesthetic world. This world, in turn, is sensible, a world whose elements – colors and form – draw their ontological substance from sensibility. To the extent that the scientific world retains an ultimate reference to the sensible world and its real determinations, it too can, through a proper use of them, be an aesthetic world. The aporia which we ran into can thus be formulated as follows: How can the work of art belong to a real world defined by sensibility and also be situated beyond it, beyond its support, in a pure imaginary?

The irreality of the work of art cannot be understood solely on the basis of its relation to the perceptual world, that is, it cannot be understood in its opposition to it, an opposition that is still immediate and naïve. Instead, it must be grasped in its original connection to the essence of life and as its main effect. If the work of art is never in this world ,if it is not truly situated where its support is – right there on this wall in front of us, in this context – *it is not that it is foreign to sensibility, but instead that its essence is located in sensibility and that its being unfolds where sensibility unfolds, in life, in the radical immanence of absolute subjectivity.* It is thus outside of the world, far away from everything that is there. It is in an "elsewhere" that every true artwork allows us to feel. This is both the elsewhere in which it stands and where we ourselves stand: it is what we are.

Art is the representation of life. Life, by its essence and the will of its innermost being, is never ex-posed or dis-posed in the ek-static Dimension of phenomenality, that is, in the appearance of a world. That is why it does not display its own reality in the world, but only is represented in it, in the form of an irreal representation and a "simple representation." And that is why art calls on the imagination, which is the faculty of representing a thing in its absence. As a representation of life, it can only actually give it as absent, as this *ens imaginarium* in which it is projected and which applies to it. It appears as if it were life. But, in this appearance in which it is given to us and in the manifest content of its appearance, it is never the appearing of life itself, that is, its auto-revelation in the sphere of the radical interiority of absolute subjectivity.

The irreality of art is thus a matter of principle. It is due to what life continually affirms about itself. It is not of the world; it cannot live in the world but only beyond it; it is what denies the world and goes beyond it. That is why the aesthetic object cannot be confused with its material support. It is this imaginary form in the dual sense that was just recognized, as the negation of objectivity itself and as the representation of life. That is why, in the end, every work of art is presented to us as an enigma, a mystery full of sense. At the root of its being, it passes through what is there and points back to an essential absence *whose being we know, however, inasmuch as we ourselves are it, inasmuch as we are not of the world, and inasmuch as we are alive.*

What we see on the walls of Daphni are in fact representations of life, representations of its essential ontological properties. We certainly need to say a little bit more here about what these properties are and about what life is in its innermost being, *in its auto-affection.* Inasmuch as it affects itself, feels itself, and experiences itself, life is completely passive in relation to its own being. It suffers itself and supports itself as something that it has neither sought nor posited, but as something that happens and continues to happen as un-willed and nonposited by the self, and yet as that which it is, as what it constantly experiences as a self. Inasmuch as life in its essence turns out to be the suffering and supporting of oneself in a suffering (*pâtir*) stronger than freedom, it is not only pathos, the passion of oneself. It is also characterized as suffering. It is the primal suffering of oneself that makes up every subjectivity grasped in its radical possibility as life – as the absolute phenomenological life that we are. The suffering of its suffering is suffering oneself and supporting oneself. Inasmuch as this suffering and supporting oneself are experiences of oneself and thus reach into oneself, seize hold of oneself through an increase of oneself and an enjoying of oneself, it thus happens to be case that, in one's feeling of oneself and in undergoing oneself, the suffering of subjectivity is also the enjoyment of subjectivity. It is a descent into one's own being, a union and communion with it in the transparency of one's affectivity.

Life in its auto-affection – in self-feeling and self-undergoing – is essentially affectivity, but affectivity is not a state or a definite and fixed tonality. It is the history of the Absolute, the infinitely varied manner in which it comes into oneself, is experienced, and embraces itself in the embrace of itself that is the essence of life. This takes place as the pathos of this embrace; it takes on as an *a priori* necessity, the fundamental ontological forms of Suffering and Joy. These are not artificial and random tonalities resulting from facts of history, but the inescapable conditions of its innermost possibility and thus of life itself. That is why Suffering and Joy are never separated, the one is the condition of the other. The suffering of oneself provides the phenomenological matter for the enjoyment of oneself. It produces the flesh out of which Joy is made. Joy, in turn, is only the phenomenological realization of this suffering and its fulfillment in the pathos of Being. It is the experience of oneself in the certitude and exaltation of oneself. One suffers and one's suffering changes into Joy, such that, in this change, each term remains as the phenomenological condition of the other and as its own substance. The absolute is historicized in each one of the fundamental ontological tonalities that constitutes its being. Each one passes into the other and inverts to it, Suffering into Joy and Despair into Beatitude. This play of the Absolute with itself is the real and veritable being of each one of us. It is the nature of each monad and is always carried out as one of them. As an auto-affection of the Absolute, the subjectivity of life is historicized and essentialized each time in the form of the Ipseity of an Individual.

We are not empirical individuals, as if we were some fragment tied to the objective world through a number of connections, delivered over to the same blind fate and just as unintelligible as it. Instead we are living beings who have the feeling of ourselves and thus, each one of us has the slow change from suffering desire into the complete fulfillment where Being allows itself to be felt in the pure joy of its Existing. That is what is written on the walls of the Byzantine monastery, and anyone could have read that there before they were mackled.

But, one might ask: if the experience of this coming into oneself through pathetic modalities has its place in the abyss of a subjectivity that does not know the ek-stasis of the world and never takes place in it – if life has no face – how could one see it on the Daphni mosaics? In truth, what do we really see on them? We do not see Suffering but a deposition, not Joy but an annunciation, not the inner change of Suffering into Joy, not the transformation of Despair into the work of salvation, but a crucifixion and a resurrection. We do not see humility – the humility of life which did not create itself and for which auto-affection is the pathos of its creation – but the washing of feet. We do not see life on the mosaics of Daphni, because objectivity is the greatest enemy of life. But we do see the figures of life. Art is the set of figures of life's essence and its fundamental properties. In all places and times, wherever it has been alive, life has provided itself with these figures. Beyond the colored tiles and the question of dating them rigorously, the essence of life is the sole and ultimate meaning of the representations drawn on the walls of Daphni. The same holds for the artistic productions of all time periods. Scientific aesthetics totally misunderstands them, and this misunderstanding opens the way for its work of death.

What science did in Daphni, it does everywhere. It does not know life, its fundamental properties, its sensibility, its pathos, or its essence. That is, it does not know *what life is for itself, what it experiences constantly, and from where it draws the hidden but invisible motivation for everything that it does.* These are the only interests that there are in the world, but their origins can never be discovered in the world, in objectivity. Without knowing life and its own interests, science is placed in a nearly inconceivable solitude. This solitude of science is technology.

Notes

1   Wassily Kandinsky, "Concerning the Spiritual in Art" in *Kandinsky: Complete Writings on Art* (Da Capo, 1994).

2   Edmund Husserl, *Ideas Pertaining to a Pure Phenomenology and a Phenomenological Philosophy: Book I*, trans. Fred Kersten (Dordrecht: Kluwer, 1983).

3 SCIENCE ALONE: TECHNOLOGY

Science, as we understand it today, is the mathematical science of nature that abstracts from sensibility. But science can only abstract from sensibility because it first abstracts from life. By proceeding in this way, it rejects and wholly misunderstands the theme of life. It is necessary to understand the reason for this misunderstanding and why science dismisses sensible qualities and no longer considers them, after it realizes its project of establishing an objective knowledge of nature. This setting aside is not obvious. Science can indeed measure the surface covered by a color. Moreover, it is able to evaluate the intensity of a color and more broadly to aim at its own being and grasp it. There is a physical theory of colors, sounds, and solids like all the other natural elements. So, why are we saying that science has set aside sensation and is not concerned with it at all? Once color or sound has become the object of scientific analysis, what is it about them that gets neglected, passed over in silence and forgotten?

It is nothing other than the being of sensation, its own reality. According to science, the being of sensations – the being of color and sound – are material movements. The determination and knowledge of these movements go together with the progress of so-called "physical" science and merges with it. The real being of sensation has nothing to do with such "movements" and the "particles" that are tied to them. It feels itself and experiences itself to such an extent that its reality consists of and is exhausted by this experience of oneself. Movements, molecules, particles, and other physical determinations lack this.

The real being of sensation does not only differ from the being of a material movement, but this difference is the greatest one conceivable, supposing that the mind can even conceive it. It is the difference or rather the

Abyss that Descartes was able to recognize, at the origin and foundation of modern thought, between the "mind" and the "body." That is to say the difference between life or what is alive, that which experiences itself and revealing itself to oneself in this mute experience of oneself, and that which cannot carry out the work of this auto-revelation and lacks it forever – it is nothing more than a "thing" and nothing other than death. By claiming to grasp the true being of sensation, the mathematical science of nature carries out a displacement or rather a skimming over of this on to a logical Abyss. It replaces the sensation of experiencing oneself itself or rather the fact itself of experiencing oneself with that which, in order to "correspond" to it in nature, to "arouse" or "provoke" it, has no relation with the subjectivity of this experience of oneself or with life.

This is what science eliminates and, along with it, everything else that comes from it and refers back to it in some way. The sensible qualities that physical theory pretends to take into account are, in the eyes of most phenomenologists, transcendent qualities of the world and objects; they are tied to them as their properties. It is the surface that is colored, the wall that is threatening, the abandoned and shadowy intersection that becomes suspect. The illusion is then to take these properties as worldly determinations and to confer exteriority onto them, as if they could find their true place and essence there, grow in it and be nourished from it, in short, *exist* as "exterior." As if there could be "color," "threat," or "suspiciousness" without this color being sensed or this threat being experienced, and as if the surface, the intersection, or the wall could be sensed or experienced in any way. It is thus not in them. These worldly determinations do not reside in the world but where something can be experienced or felt: in what feels and experiences itself in order to be able to feel and experience anything else. The scientific attempt to reduce the lifeworld to a world of idealities and physical-mathematical abstractions is based on the prior illusion that the sensible properties of the world are its own and belong to it and that, since color is in nature and not in the mind, its natural being can be grasped by a more refined analysis than that of perception, by a physical analysis.

This reduction of the lifeworld to the world of science can only be prohibited by a thought that can grasp the lifeworld in its specificity, that is to say, as strange as it might seem, in its irreducibility to the world and to any possible world. The lifeworld is a sensible world, and sensible-being ultimately resides outside of the world, in life itself. Sensible qualities are always only the objectification and thus the re-presentation of an impression whose impressional-being is the auto-impression, that is, absolute subjectivity as life.

Here we discover the insufficiency of the classical approach of phenomenology. It takes the opposite course from Galilean science and carries out a questioning back from the world of science to the lifeworld and then from it to the consciousness of this world. Consciousness of the world is "consciousness of," intentionality, and ultimately the ek-stasis of Being in which intentionality is deployed in turn. It does not allow for the collection of sensation into oneself and thus its coming into being. Instead, in the opening up of ek-stasis, sensation is cast outside itself, disposed and dispersed as a "representational sensation." It is the humus of this world as the lifeworld, and as a result, this representational sensation can only ever be the irreal representation of the real sensation whose reality is found in auto-sensation, not in the consciousness of the world but in life.

This is what our brief analysis of the work of art had already shown. Those who follow the brilliant suggestions of Husserl and reduce it to a pure imaginary (thus distinguishing it from its support which alone belongs to the world of perception) draw the conclusion that the real world is not beautiful on its own and could not be so – it is neither beautiful nor ugly. If that were the case, the ransacking of the earth by technology would be without gravity or even might not happen at all. For how could one ever disfigure and plunge into the horrible something whose nature would escape from every aesthetic category?

Another consequence of the thesis of the imaginary status of the work of art would be equally contestable. For, if the artwork were a pure imaginary and were exhausted in it in the same way as any other image, one would search in vain for some foundation to attribute its internal coherence, and thereby its readability, to the rigorous determination of its parts as elements of the aesthetic composition. We have shown that these elements are already aesthetic on their own. What characterizes the ordinary image is that it is sustained at each moment by the imaginative act of the consciousness that posits it, and it is only the end result of this activity. It does not suffer any passivity of the regard and collapses when the conscious act that produces it is interrupted. I cannot, as Sartre says, count the number of columns on the Pantheon that I form an image of.

One of the remarkable features of the artwork is the clarity and precision of its details. In the "Deposition of Christ" by Fra Angelico at the National Museum of San Marco, I can count the number of characters in the foreground, the number of towers in the enclosure, the number of houses or buildings seen above the wall, etc. Their rigorous placement, the evidence and the constraining force of the internal relations of the composition make it into what it is.

More significant still is the manner in which it is given to us. It is not given as an ontological deficiency, like the fragile result of an activity without which it would sink immediately into nothingness but as the massive imposition of what, through its own consistency, exerts the power of putting us in the situation of being a *spectator* of it – that is, a wholly passive being with regard to what is given to be contemplated. As our earlier analyses suggested, this is because the site of the artwork is not first an imaginary noema constituted beyond the support but subjectivity itself. Subjectivity is the place where every sensation and image is formed, where they increase on their own and thereby support themselves, succumbing under the weight of their own being. Each objective element of the composition – the support and the image neutralize one another in the specific dimension of the work – corresponds to a specific affective tonality in which each thing that is seen, imagined and felt is auto-affected. This is the emotion evoked by the canvas, statue or monument: that is what the creator sought to express and what the spectator feels. The spectator thereby coincides with the essence of art.

But if, as an auto-affection of the ek-stasis of Being, the work of art has the same status as the sensible world, in what way does it differ from it? It differs in that it is an organized world whose elements are used and composed in order to produce more intense and determined sentiments, the very same ones, as we just saw, that the artist wants to express. Or rather, nature is a distended work whose effect, that is to say the perception of it, is only beautiful to a weaker degree, in an accidental but yet essential way, if it is true that it is sensible and as such aesthetic. It obeys the laws of sensibility which are the laws of the constitution of every possible world.

Abstracting from the sensible-lifeworld does not only put out of play the sensible qualities of the world but, at the same time, life itself. When thought through to its end, we can then discover the solitude of science, a solitude that is so extreme that it is almost unimaginable. Science, as we will show, never exists alone. But once it has cast life outside of its field of investigations (and it necessarily does this as science), it acts *as if* it were alone. Hence, it will dictate its own laws to the world – to the sensible lifeworld that remains, even though it has abstracted from everything that is sensible and alive. This situation – in which a theoretical decision (*instance*) will determine the lifeworld and life itself without considering them in any way – characterizes the current phase of world history. We can say that we are undergoing Modernity, if it is true that in Modernity, for the first time ever, life has ceased to dictate its own laws for itself.

When science takes itself to be alone in the world and acts in that way, it becomes technology. It is a set of operations and transformations that become possible through science and its theoretical knowledge, to the exclusion of any reference to the lifeworld and life itself. Yet, due to its dual relation, positive with regard to science but negative with regard to life, the essence of technology is difficult to grasp. A systematic elucidation of it is thus necessary.

Interpretations of technology have rightly increased in an era where everyone can perceive the profound changes affecting the world and also have a vague sense of the immense threat hanging over our lives. These interpretations can be divided into two groups. Some see modern technology as the gradual affirmation of the mastery of humans over the world of things, for technology is no more than a set of increasingly numerous, sophisticated, and powerful tools. Through its means and ends, they refer to humanity's higher interests and, through the use of all the new possibilities offered by science, they will finally have the opportunity to be realized. Can "progress" mean anything but this gradual realization of the highest ends of humanity, ends that are its own and constitutive of its essence, by science?

Unfortunately, when it comes to these "higher interests" of "humanity" itself, that is to say of the essence of life, science and the technology that stems from it do not know anything about them and do not consider them at all. That is why, if one is speaking about the "means" of technology, one must realize that one is talking about a very specific type of means. They are no longer in the service of an end that is different from themselves; instead, they themselves constitute the "end." We thus find ourselves in the presence of an impressive array of instrumental devices and operations. The means of production are increasingly effective and sophisticated processes. Since their development is not stimulated or governed by anything else, it thus occurs as an auto-development. In the auto-development of a system of processes based on the theoretical knowledge of science, these processes are delivered over to themselves, play by and for themselves, and answer to this knowledge. Consequently, instead of letting themselves be determined by it, they arouse and give rise to it, as its true cause. That is the essence of modern technology.

Which of these two conceptions of technology is the best one? How can one choose between them? Would they not both be true in their own ways, if they were connected to an essential history of technology and to crucial moments appearing in this history – each one of these "interpretations" would correspond to certain moments as a more or less happy representation of these moments, as the ideology of an epoch? But this history can only be an essential history, if it goes back to the origin of *techne*, that is to say, to its true essence, to the possibility of something being a "technology" as well as the different phases of this development. These phases are not chance or contingent, as the vicissitudes and events of what is generally called history. They are necessary inasmuch as they are rooted in the original essence of *techne*. They are made possible and required by it.

Here we find ourselves in the midst of an extraordinary situation. In order to understand the various forms of technology, we must bring into view the original essence of *techne* and in particular the essence of modern technology that abstracts from life, but this original essence is life itself. "Technology" refers generally to "know-how," but the original essence of technology is not a particular type of know-how. It is "know-how" as such. This knowledge consists of making, that is to say, it is a making that carries its own knowledge within itself and constitutes it. Making is able to constitute this type of knowing and be identified with it, inasmuch as it feels itself and experiences itself in each point of its being. It is a radically subjective making that draws its essence from subjectivity and becomes possible through it. Any "know-how" whatsoever, in its various forms, contains within itself this original knowledge whose essence is doing and ultimately the subjectivity of doing. The original "know-how" is praxis. It is thus life itself, since praxis is known in life. The original essence of technology resides in this original "know-how." So, on the basis of life, how can we understand the emergence of a process from which life will be chased way and that, as a system of devices and objective processes, is undertaking the devastation of its lifeworld right before our eyes?

The original essence of *techne* is not an ideal essence floating somewhere in front of us in intelligible space: this is only the case in the eyes of theory. As an auto-affecting praxis, it is determined and individualized in and through auto-affection. Everything that is felt and experienced necessarily feels itself and experiences itself not only in this or that way but as this or that. Consequently, it is a *singular* experience, and by nature, this is an *individual* experience, if it is the case that the essence of auto-affection is ipseity. This determinate praxis, as singular and individual, is our Body.

Its force is auto-affected and continually auto-affects itself. In the exercise of this force, the body runs up against a first resistance. Its internal phenomenological systems give way to its effort and constitute our "organic body." These are not our group of "organs" as they appear to an objective knowledge of some kind but precisely as we live them within our subjective body as the terms of our effort. These are the primal "configurations" whose entire being consists in their being-given-to effort and exhausted in it. Second, at the very heart of this zone of relative resistance offered by the organic body, the pressure that weighs on it and gradually makes it give way, that is, the use of the powers of the subjective body, runs up against an obstacle that no longer gives way. The Earth is a line of absolute resistance that lets itself be felt continually within the organic body and is the unsurpassable limit of its deployment. Here again, the Earth is as we live it, that is to say as we experience it in our subjective bodily movement. It exists in the effort that pushes it back, defeats it, and breaks it apart.

The original essence of *techne* is the whole system formed by my body in movement and effort. My immanent Body is absolutely subjective and absolutely alive – the organic body that exerts itself and bends under its effort. In turn, the Earth refuses to bend and is opposed to effort – it is given as that which can no longer be defeated or be forced to give way. The radically immanent subjective Body in which I stand as the fundamental "I Can" has such difficultly that I am the task of making the Earth give way and move back. This occurs through the use of its own powers, and this is why tools were invented. That is to say, elements of the Earth were taken away from it in order to be turned against it. They were used in order to dig, move and modify the Earth in multiple ways and to give it a new form. The "tool" is originally nothing but an extension of the immanent subjective Body. It is thus a part of the organic body. That is, something that gives way to effort and is given in and only in that way. It is what happens to the making of a movement. It is what is taken, moved, handled and manipulated by it. Its substance is derived from being its moving term, its practical, unstable, and problematic limit. Its determination and fixation are left to the power of this movement. The tool is detached from nature in order to be delivered over to the initiative of the Body and put to use by it.

This "detachment," however, is only apparent; it only underscores a feature of nature. By its essence, nature is available to an original Body, that is, either the fluctuating correlate of a movement or its fixed limit. This "fixity" is determined only in and through this movement. The Earth is not conceivable except as that on which we place or can place our feet, as the ground on which we stand. The "air" is not conceivable except as that which we breathe or that which might burn us. No surface, volume or solid is conceivable except the one that we can touch. No light is conceivable except the one that shines in the subjectivity of our Eye. Body and Earth are joined together by Co-belonging (*Copropriation*). It is so original that nothing can ever occur in a pure Outside, as an object, for a *theoria*, as something that would be there without us – except as the history of this original Co-belonging (*Copropriation*) and as its limit mode. We will call this original Co-belonging (*Copropriation*) a Bodily-ownness (*Corpspropriation*). It is so original that it makes us the owners of the world. This does not occur after the fact due to a decision of our own or a given society's adoption of a specific behavior toward the cosmos. It is *a priori*, in virtue of the corporeal condition of our "Bodily-ownness" (*corps-proprié*). We transform the world. The history of humanity is the history of this transformation, to such a point that it is impossible to look at a field without seeing in it the effect of some kind of praxis. But the transformation of the world is only the use and actualization of the Bodily-ownness (*Corpspropriation*) that makes us inhabit the Earth as its owners. What we are now beginning to understand a little better is the way in which the world is always initially the lifeworld. We are beginning to understand a little better that *before even being a sensible world, the world is the correlate of the movement of a Bodily-ownness (corps-proprié).*

All the difficulties concerning the intelligence of praxis arise from thought. They arise as soon as one thinks about representing it, instead of living the inner development of the organic body in the subjective tension of the original Body. It then becomes necessary to understand how a subjective determination can change a natural being – how the "mind" can act on the "body." This question is all the more unsolvable when moving from one dimension of being – where action is merely exercised – to another one, the sphere of "objectivity" where action was never produced and will never occur. The "mind," the subjective body, became thought, that is to say, representation, and as a result, the way to approach praxis as subjective and living vanishes.

The representation of praxis gives rise to the ideology that interprets technology as the instrumental transformation of nature by ends that are posited by human beings. On the one hand, this ideology represents the original Co-belonging (*Co-propriation*) of the Body and the Earth within the core of Life. On the other hand, as a representation, life is seriously altered in the following ways: 1) by taking action outside of its proper ontological milieu, it renders action unintelligible; 2) by breaking the inner unity of the immanent deployment of the organic body, it projects the notions of "cause," "effect," "means," and "ends" as disjunctive elements in the exteriority of representation. The relations between them become unintelligible when the categories of rational thought are used in place of those of the Body. If such a conception of technology, however, turns out to be completely inappropriate today, it is not merely because it carries out a displacement of praxis from the place of its real fulfillment through its falsifying representation in an understanding that posits causes and ends. It is because an overturning occurred in this place of its real accomplishment, in the subjectivity of life, and this overturning threatens the foundations of Being.

As long as it overlaps with individual spontaneous praxis, *techne* is simply the expression of life. It is the use of the powers of the subjective body and thus one of the primary forms of culture. The internal demands of life give rise to it, and these demands can then be represented as its "causes" or its "ends." The phenomenological structures of the original body determine the modalities of its exercise, or rather, they *are* these modalities. If this primitive activity must still be adapted to nature, this adaptation proceeds from itself. For, true Nature is Bodily-ownness (*corps-propriée*), and action or elementary work is only the actualization of this Bodily-ownness (*Corpspropriation*). The higher forms of culture such as art, ethics or religion are also modes of *techne*. There the determination of praxis by life is even more evident to the extent that the moral or religious *habitus* as well as aesthetic creation are direct and immediate expressions of living subjectivity. Their principle resides in them and their forms of regulation. It is the place where they come into being, that is, their concrete modalities of realization.

The ontological revolution occurs when action ceases to obey the prescriptions of life and it is no longer what it was at the beginning, that is, the actualization of the phenomenological potential of absolute subjectivity. Moreover, it seems that action has deserted the site that was always its own in order to take place in the world henceforth: in factories, dams, and power plants. It is now wherever there are pistons, turbines, cogs and all kinds of machines that fire away all the time. In short, it is the immense mechanical system of big industry, which can be reduced to the electromagnetic currents of supercomputers and other high-tech machines of "techno-science." This points to the crucial event of Modernity in the passage from the reign of the human to the nonhuman: *action has become objective.* The surface of the Earth now resembles its physico-mathematical sub-layer: the whirling of atoms, the collisions of particles, and the age-old, frenetic restlessness of bio-evolution that occurs without any origin, cause, or aim.

We are only saying that "it seems this way" because in fact action is only possible in and through subjectivity as a praxis. It is only in the radical immanence of its original corporeity that the body takes hold and makes use of its powers so that they can "serve" oneself when one wants them to. Once this placement within oneself that is characteristic of all power and doing ceases, and once subjectivity no longer provides its essence as auto-affection, "action" would no longer take place. There would only remain physical movements, like the fall of water in the waterfall, the various mechanisms of industry, the phenomena of propagation, or the "trajectories" of micro-physics. The content of modern technology is only made up of this kind of objective processes that occur on their own, as in cybernetics or the micro-physical substrate of the universe. In short, it is made up of a set of devices that are no longer living and are no longer life. This is what it always deals with and what constitutes its being; it is the fabric out of which it is made and its "substance."

Such processes do not happen to seem "blind," since they culminate in coherent and finalized results. In the case of technology, they are the results of knowledge. *But of what kind of knowledge?* Here is the ontological reversal brought about by the modern Era or, to put it in a more neutral way, the major "revolution" that occurred in the "history of human kind." Let us set aside the political revolutions that are only the consequences or symptoms of it. One draws near to the essential point with Marx, when one can recognize the inversion of vital teleology that occurred at the end of the eighteenth and nineteenth centuries. The production of consumer goods that is characteristic of every society ceased to be directed by and for their "use value" in order to then see the obtaining and growth of the exchange value, that is to say, money. When production *became economic* and acted for the sake of making money – that is to say, when an economic reality took the place of goods useful for life and designated for it – the entire face of the world was changed.

Original nature defined as Bodily-ownness (*Corpspropriation*) realizes itself in the actualization of the subjective potential of living Corporeity, and in fact, it is this actualization. This lifeworld is not the world of intuition but the world of praxis. It is the world as the effect of praxis but, more essentially, as its exercise. It is the world not as an Object but as Action; its Action is the Body. On the one hand, this world had to be severely disrupted by the emergence of a purpose without any relation to what it is and has always been – namely, by the production of an abstraction: the production of money. A similar disruption occurs with the appearance and development a new ontological dimension – economic reality – that does not belong primordially to corporeal nature or to the Body itself. On the other hand, production changes altogether once it is the production of money and no longer of use values. It is no longer being motivated, defined and limited by the potentialities of subjectivity – by "needs" – its ends are no longer found there. This amounts to saying that it is no longer *in itself* the fulfillment of these potentialities. They thereby cease to be qualitatively differentiated and become quantitative, "infinite," like the money that they produce.

This "economic revolution" is not a revolution within the preexisting economic world; instead, it is its emergence and introduction into being. This is not the one and only revolution that came along to subvert the Bodily-ownness (*Corpsporpiation*) that defines the original condition of humans on the earth and thus their history. It only paved the way for it, acting as its cause but not its true essence. For economic reasons (such as the need to maintain profit margins and surplus-value), the frenetic acceleration of production as economic production gives rise to innovation, the proliferation of new means of production, and the perfecting of older ones. An extraordinary development of technology results. It makes scientific inventions profitable and, in turn, gives rise to more of them. The means of production is no longer the "tool" that extends the subjective body and is predefined by it, whose handling is only the use of the powers of this body, its exercise, and as a result, a fundamental form of culture. This "means," this "tool," has become the mechanical, objective network that functions on its own in the machine, in industry, in cybernetics and perhaps in nature itself, at least as nature appears in the eyes of the moderns. What happens in such a change?

The knowledge that makes action possible and regulates it is no longer the knowledge of life but that of science. That is the radical revolution that has come to undermine the humanity of the human being and looms with the greatest threat that has been encountered since the beginning of time. When the knowledge that regulates action is the knowledge of life, life coincides with action and is nothing but its auto-affection. We have characterized this type of knowledge that resides in doing as the essence of all know-how. That is why it is part of every form of activity, particularly those that are called "instinctive": the primal relation of the Earth and the human being, the possibility of standing on its ground, walking, working, erotic behavior, the use of the senses, movement, and all the various powers of subjectivity (imagination, memory, etc.). All these activities are the fulfillment of life, its self-realization and self-growth, its culture.

When scientific knowledge regulates action, its results are the following. First, the nature of knowledge is completely changed. It is no longer knowledge of life but consciousness of objects. Moreover, this form of objective knowledge abstracts from the senses as well as the existence of the sensible qualities in the world that it knows. Second, this knowledge is no longer action in itself and no longer coincides with it. Third, it is not the knowledge *of* action either, an objective knowledge of it, because action is not and cannot be objective. Such knowledge has really become the knowledge of an objectivity, that is to say, of a natural process reduced by science to its abstract and ideal parameters, to the physico-mathematical determinations of the world of Galilean science. Acting and knowing – identified with science – henceforth fall outside of one another. Action is no longer anything but a sort of empirical curiosity, the "action" by which the scientist moves his or her eyeballs or turns the pages of his or her book. Or, it slips from view and is not even taken into consideration, and thus it is nothing. Knowledge, by contrast, is everything. It is scientific knowledge in its continual theoretical development. Its correlate is all objective processes, including the processes of the instrumental network of industry, cybernetics, and of nature itself. The knowledge of science, or more precisely the science of nature, now defines the knowledge of *techne*, instead of the knowledge of life. But, if *techne* is the condition of possibility of every conceivable action, if action resides in praxis, and if the essence of praxis resides in life and the original Bodily-ownness (*Corpspropriation*) of nature, how then is modern technology – that is to say, the information and transformation of the world by science – conceivable? How would the knowledge of science – a purely theoretical gaze – be capable of "acting" on the objective processes of nature that have become the instrumental networks of industry and machines in general? We have recognized the insolubility of the problem of the relation between the "mind" – reduced to a theoretical gaze – and the "body," understood as a natural being and an object.[1]

Let us just say here that if science is capable of making the slightest material modification to nature, this is only insofar as a real action cannot be reduced to a merely theoretical relation between a knowing subject and a known object. In reality, it always takes the unperceived detour through Bodily-ownness (*Corpspropriation*). Only someone who has hands and eyes in the sense of a radically immanent power of grasping and seeing, only a being originally constituted in oneself as a subjective and living Body – only the scientist not as a scientist but as this kind of being – can turn the pages of a book and read it. Likewise, only such a person can carry out a scientific operation of any kind: handle a tool, press a button, follow the results of a change on a graph, and then understand the results of a sophisticated experiment. These results are ultimately offered as sensible givens, and they are only accessible in that form. The same goes for experimentation properly so-called. The conduct or handling of it always refers back to and presupposes an action of the original Body.

This situation does not only hold for scientific practice; it also determines the condition of the worker in the modern world. What characterizes the modern worker is the gradual decrease of the role of living work, or subjective praxis, in the real process of production, whereas the role of the objective, instrumental network continually increases, first in the form of machines in a traditional big industry and later cybernetics and robotics. The law of the gradual decrease of profit margins in the capitalist era is only the expression on the economic level of the crucial phenomenon that has come to affect modern production: the invasion of technology and its expulsion of life.

Even when production tends to be identified with technical devices and thus with technology itself, the decreasing role of living work within it signifies nothing but this. As in the case of pure science, the transformation of the world presupposes a prior access to the objective processes of nature

investment in an actual process of production, its exchange against the use-value of raw materials and machines, and even more essentially, against the living work that is alone able to put into play this entire process and to produce the exchange value through it. This clearly shows that money never stands on its own. Even when it defines a new economic end in capitalism, it is always obligated to change into its contrary and to return to its source in life. At the end of the process, this is imposed again through the consumption that production cannot do without. In spite of everything, the stimulation of artificial consumption and the creation of new needs to absorb this production that has been deregulated by exchange value is controlled by artificial needs and, through them, by the subjectivity of life. That was still, even in the eyes of Marx, a way of developing and enriching life, *an element of culture.*

We said above that all production is derived from consumption and cannot do without it. The exchange value that is produced in capitalism can only come into being through a use value whose nature and properties are determined by subjectivity. This imposes, in the very heart of a value system, a teleology that cannot totally be thrown away and that roots this entire process in an ontology of life. *This rootedness is broken in the technological world.* The process of production no longer gets its ultimate rationale from the use value and life. Instead, it precedes it in a state of affairs where life is absent and where it is never taken into consideration, either as a cause, an end, or even a means. What, then, is the state of affairs from which all production proceeds in the technological world, if this production has emptied praxis from itself and constantly seeks to do so, and if it is reduced to an objective process?

It is the prior state of the instrumental network, that is, all of the technologies existing at a given moment. On the basis of them, it is possible to build new ones whose nature is predetermined by all of the preexisting technologies and the scientific knowledge at the time. Such a possibility is much more than a possibility. Since all that exists is the state of affairs defined by this set of technologies and the scientific knowledge that overlaps with it, this state of affairs will decide the "future" of its own development. And that is how, through a multiplicity of objective processes scientifically defined and based, every new device and every technology is implied in some way by the system of existing technologies. They result from their interconnection and relationships. Whatever can be conceived and realized through them and whatever possibilities they contain will exist for sure. This invincible movement is called progress.

The notion of progress has thus come to designate technological progress exclusively. The idea of aesthetic, intellectual, spiritual or moral progress –

which would be situated in the life of the individual and consisting in the self-development and self-growth of multiple phenomenological potentialities of life and its culture – is obsolete. It no longer has any identifiable place in the implicit ontology of our times, where the only reality is objective and scientifically knowable. Technological progress was traditionally understood as the result of a "brilliant" theoretical discovery, that is to say, of something accomplished by an exceptional individual like Pasteur. But its nature too has completely changed. The life and path of the individual activity of the inventor was connected back to the progress of culture in general and understood as one of its offshoots. But nothing like that can be found today in the development of the technology that carries out its own self-development. All that can be said is that if technologies *a, b, c* are the givens that lead to the technology *d*, this latter will be produced inevitably as their result; it does not matter by whom or where. This explains the simultaneity of discoveries in various countries as well as their inevitability. Their "application" is not the contingent and possible result of a prior theoretical content; it is already an "application," an instrumental device, a technology. Besides, no authority (*instance*) exists that would be different from this device and from the scientific knowledge materializing in it that would decide whether or not it should be "realized." The technological world thus spreads like a cancer. It produces and guides itself, in the absence of any norms, in its perfect indifference toward everything that is not itself – toward life.

With its seemingly autonomous laws, its abstract purposes, its incomprehensible contradictions, its unforeseeable effects, economic development constituted a specific world. It was experienced by human beings as a foreign destiny. It distributed alternately either prosperity or misery, and most often misery. Yet, this fate derived its substance from their own lives, their work, hopes, and sufferings, even if it turned against them, in an incomprehensible way, to crush and subjugate them. With technology, the autonomous feature of development ceased to be a mere appearance. It is a movement that has no relation to life. It neither asks anything from it nor gives anything to it, nothing that resembles it in any case or conforms in any way to its essence or wishes. What it brings to life, or what it imposes on life, is *the other of life*. These are procedures and mechanisms buried in nature, which science extracts from its bosom. It tears them away from the obscure Ends in which they are shrouded and delivers them over to themselves, in their abstraction and isolation. They are then disconnected and joined only by artificial connections: set alongside one another, added to one another, in a random order that is no longer that of Nature or Life. It is no longer an order at all but a savage process in which every new possibility born from a fortuitous encounter becomes the sole reason for a development that no longer has any reason. Freed from every connection, separated from every coherent and purposive totality, technology marches ahead, straight ahead, like an interplanetary rocket, without knowing where it comes from, where it is going, or why. In its radical exteriority to life – to the life that feels and experiences itself and draws from what it experiences in it the laws for its action and development – it has become an absolute transcendence, without reason and without light, without a face and without a regard, a "dark transcendence."[2]

Even if we were to suppose that, within this monstrous development of modern technology, the appearance of a new procedure – the splitting of the atom, genetic modification, etc. – would raise any questions to the conscience of the scientist, such a question would be swept aside as anachronistic. There is no longer any questioning or conscience in the only reality that exists for science. And if by chance a scientist were to be stopped by his or her scruples – which never would happen because the scientist is in the service of science – hundreds of others would rise up and come along to take up the torch. Everything that can be done by science ought to be done by it and for it, since there is nothing but science and the reality that it knows, namely, objective reality. Technology is its self-realization.

Notes

1   It is quite remarkable that Cartesianism did not face this problem and only came up against it when it was approached in a theoretical way, that is to say, "scientific" and objective, in the *Passions of the Soul*. So long as Descartes held to the phenomenological reduction, a reduction that the analyses of the present work are also operating within, the action of the body did not present any difficulty. Its possibility had been resolved automatically. That is the reason why one can say that Descartes provides an admirable anticipation of the conception of the subjective body, as seen in his Reply to Five Objections. There he mentions an "*ambulandi cogitatio,*" that is to say, of the original subjective experience of walking. See Descartes, *Oeuvres VII*, 352.

2   Gilbert Hottois, *Le Signe et la Technique* (Paris: Aubier, 1984), 152.

4 THE SICKNESS OF LIFE

Does science really not have any relation to life? By tearing away the ineffable singularity of sensible and individual beings and making them disappear, the Galilean approach reduces the being of things in order to posit them instead as stable-beings that can be known by all, a being that is in itself and objective. Hasn't the critique of the scientific world – that is to say of science itself inasmuch as it only knows its own world – shown that these mathematical idealities, instead of putting subjectivity out of play and delivering us from it, are produced by it and refer back to it as their inevitable presupposition and foundation? But if subjectivity were considered as the power of creating these scientific idealities and as a consciousness that bestows sense, as an intentional "consciousness of," subjectivity is also always something else, that is, life itself. It is the original auto-affection of this creative sense bestowal to the idealities of mathematical physics.

But, in the reduction, must not the regard that we cast on science – we phenomenologists who are careful to construct a radical phenomenology of subjectivity as a living subjectivity, that is to say, to preserve the being that we really are beyond all appearances – be considerably altered? Science does not simply abstract from the lifeworld and consequently from life itself. This abstraction is the putting out of play of sensible qualities, and it is the constitutive operation of modern science in its initial and founding reasoning. This operation, as we said, is an operation of absolute subjectivity, and in this way, a mode of life. Even though science separates life from its thematic and no matter how much it misunderstands life, it nonetheless remains – in its inaugural act as well as each of its subsequent steps – a modality of this absolute life and belongs to it.

Along with the regard that we cast onto it, what also changes is the situation of science in relation to the domain of culture. As long as we only consider the modern scientific *intentio* and it alone, we are only concerned about nature reduced to its abstract mathematical determinations – about a nature whose subjective properties have been removed. Taking this scientifically determined being to be essential and more over taking it as the sole being that really exists and that can be known in a rigorous and universally valid way, we take everything that is not it to be nothing at all, including the phenomenologically absolute life. To the degree that culture is the culture of life and concerns it alone, a science that separates its thematic from life and its specific development in culture remains entirely foreign to culture. The relation between science and culture is a relation of mutual exclusion. The example of art offered proof of this exclusion and also pushed it to its greatest extreme. Art gives expression to sensibility and investigates its most meaningful accomplishments, whereas science eliminates this very same sensibility, which is to say both the life world and life itself, and places itself paradoxically outside of life and its development. As a consequence, it is outside of all culture.

This exclusion, however, is only the case in the eyes of science and its intention not to consider sensibility. Science is unable to keep this *intentio* – the radicality of its Galilean project – inasmuch as these idealities inevitably refer to a sensible given. And moreover, even when it pursues the continual constitution of these physico-mathematical idealities, we have seen that its activity is still a subjective activity. Even if it is never offered to the aim of science and is never the theme of its investigations, this does not keep it from being realized. This achievement already shows, in the completion of its operation, that science does not dominate all of reality and does not display it entirely in the field of its objects and theories. It has let something essential escape, nothing less than its own foundation.

If we consider more closely this foundation that science never considers, and if we relate it explicitly to its ontological dimension, that is to absolute subjectivity, we are then forced to reverse the relation between science and culture. This relation no longer appears to us in the form of their mutual exclusion but of their reciprocal adherence. The self-assigned task of traditional philosophy was to contrast science, its activity and concrete productions, with the transcendental conditions of its own possibility. Since science was so preoccupied with its own work, it did not have time to examine those conditions itself. Philosophy would then show that even the most advanced and abstract knowledge occurs within an initial access to the world and that this prior openness is presupposed. This was constituted by the *a priori* forms of intuition and the categories of the understanding and ultimately by the Ek-stasis of being that is the basis of them, in turn. The transcendental condition of the possibility of any experience whatsoever is the condition of science itself. There is a division of labor between the philosopher and the scientist. The philosopher reflects on the most general conditions of a concrete and ever changing work, while the scientist is devoted to and absorbed in doing this work.

But, in classical thought and its contemporary developments, subjectivity is reduced to the condition of the possibility of the object and thus to objectivity considered as such; it is reduced to the original Outside without which it is said that nothing would exist. When this occurs, it is philosophy as well as science that get cast outside of culture. The fragile alliance between them only served to lead them into the same abyss. This happens inasmuch as culture is the culture of life and is only intelligible on the basis of life. But when subjectivity is nothing more than exteriority and its deployment, when it is no longer something alive and that by which it is alive has been lost from view, denied or hidden, by philosophy as well as science, then philosophy has no lesson to teach science. They both live in the same forgetting, in the same stupor in front of what is there in front of them. It is all that can be said to exist in their eyes. The philosophical critique of science has lost all of its identifiable content. One can indeed denounce modern theory, as a theory reduced to technology, to the manipulation and calculation of being. But it is necessary to recall that "through theory in the modern sense there is the shadow of the original *theoria*"[1] and that the ontological milieu where they are produced by first producing the world is the Same. It is the Ek-stasis of the Outside where nothing is alive.

To conceive the relation between science and culture, it is insufficient to underscore the subjective nature of scientific activity as such and especially its Galilean origin – that is, the proto-act by which consciousness replaces the empirical given with its geometrical idealization and for which this idealization as such is constituted as the correlate of a specific invention and creation. This subjectivity must also be understood as life. The transcendental acts that either make or are science can be understood as modalities of absolute life, just like artistic creations, for example. They are cultural phenomena, just like artistic phenomena are.

To say that the operations of scientific subjectivity are modalities of life means that, although they are put out of play by the Galilean reduction along with everything else that is subjective and subjectivity itself in general, they nonetheless exist as they are and with their own properties. They are experiences in the sense of life. They are not simply intentions directed toward idealities with their rules and implications. These scientific intentionalities affect themselves and are only possible on that basis. The seeing that sees in them and knows is a seeing that feels its own seeing. Seeing experiences itself as seeing and can only see on this condition and in this way. It is thus not a mere metaphor to speak about a scientific life, about the life of the scientist as a scientist, as if it were only an allusion to an empirical companion of science itself, an addition to its own being – an addition due to the contingent fact that science is done by human beings, after all. This science – like all knowing and all seeing – is only possible as life. It cannot be absorbed into the objective world of its objects and theories. In spite of their objectivity and universality, all of its products are products in the strict sense of the term. They refer to a transcendental life without which they could not exist.

Because scientific acts are alive and are thus experiences in an original sense, they are necessarily actualized by specific modalities. Each is what it is, with its own tonality and its difference from all the others. They are not simply ideal intuitions, inferences, hypotheses, premises, or conclusions that can all be placed under an eidetic typology that gives predicative life its own style. Each one of the acts corresponding to these types is also a singular act, with its own individuality that is both similar and different from all the other ones that obey the same laws. Once again, the fact that the scientist does not pay attention to the particularity of this experience does not change anything about its reality. Instead, this misunderstanding ought to lead us to reflect on the status of this experience and on the reasons why it is never taken into consideration, even though it supports the entire scientific edifice. This happens because it never stands in the foreground of the light in which science and consciousness find their objects; it is never offered as one of them. The radical immanence of life and everything that belongs to it – especially the living modalities of scientific activity which never appear in the horizon of transcendence and are never an object – takes them away from scientific and philosophical reflection.

As living modalities of absolute subjectivity, scientific sense-bestowals are not simply some of its own features, as its undeniable acts. They are not some sort of transcendental fact to a higher degree – something that must be known in order to be able to do this. Nor are they "essences" or some sort of data or opaque properties of this life. They are its possibilities. Life lives in them and holds them as its own powers, as *what it can do and as nothing apart from this ability to do.*

Inasmuch as they are the phenomenological potentialities of life, essences are not first offered as the correlates of an eidetic intuition. It is a mistake to grant them the ability to make manifest and thus to posit them initially in being. The original essences are not ideal or transcendent. They are the primal, practical determinations of life, and in this respect they are not givens, the object of a seeing or the correlate of a *theoria*. They are potentialities. Being is essentialized as a praxis and in this form alone, as a determination of it.

It is precisely because the original essences – the essences of conception, ideation, and abstraction – are modalities of praxis and thus of life itself that life is able to deploy them. It keeps them always at its disposal, as its own possibilities, and it leads into action each time, as often as it likes. An object is something that one can catch sight of, analyze, thematize, or turn away from. Conceiving, idealizing, abstracting, contemplating, analyzing, thematizing and so forth – life is only able to carry out all of these operations of scientific knowledge, because it is identified with them. The essence which they actualize is its own essence, that with which it is identified, of which it defines the real-being, *auto-affection*, such that it coincides with these fundamental capacities of intelligence and can use them.

The operations of science are modalities of absolute life in the sense just mentioned, that is, as the exercise of life's potential, their being put to use and put to the test. Their practical-being is carried into this practice and comes to its highest possible degree of realization, to its fulfillment and its growth, through it. To this degree, science thus understood – not in a restrictive way as the field of its ideal objectivities but on the basis of the transcendental sense-bestowals that produce it and that are the actualization of the original phenomenological potentialities of absolute subjectivity – is in its full concreteness nothing other than a form of culture.

It gets its ontological site – praxis – from culture, as well as the characteristics of a "reality" defined by and as practice. These are as follows. First, the characteristic of not being a substance or a thing but the realization of a potentiality, whose ultimate essence is found in the possibility of all potentiality: in auto-affection. Second, the characteristic of a becoming that is due to the fact that every actualization is more or less perfect and that, through its continual repetition, it leads to a *habitus* that has been acquired and underlies subsequent actualizations. It is not just the sensible eye that can be either crude or refined. The capacity to grasp idealities, to subsume a sensible given under an ideal relation that can explain it and connect it, for example, to a type that explains its properties and thus illuminates it in a clearer way – this ability too is part of the history of progress. Its mode of fulfillment is a mode of exercise; it is a practical mode. In this regard, the mind – by this, I mean specifically absolute subjectivity's set of potentialities for knowing – is exactly like what Descartes wanted. It is an *ingenium*, that is, the continual exercise of the potentialities of the theoretical regard in increasingly rigorous and certain modes. Science, in its founding possibility, is connected with this *ingenium*. It is one of the concrete modes of the life of absolute subjectivity, as a knowing life and thus as a fundamental form of culture.

As a mode of life and consequently as a way of living, science is more or less analogous to other forms of culture, both to its immediate forms in the daily praxis of work and need as well as the higher products of art, ethics or religion. These are all modes of realizing life. Life seeks the fulfillment of these modes, inasmuch as it is ultimately the growth of the self. Yet, when it adopts the characteristics of culture and seeks to play a leading role in the modern world, science presents a singular feature which differentiates it from the other manifestations of the mind. In a certain sense, this forces a choice between them. We need to return to this singular feature, which has already been glimpsed above.

Science – the mathematical science of nature – put out of play the sensible qualities of nature, that is, the lifeworld and life itself. It is not at all concerned about the fact that this science is carried out as a modality of life, and consequently as a form of culture, as we have said. The putting out of play of life then takes on two different meanings. The weaker one results from the recognition of a fact: by thematizing nature as reduced to its ideal determinations, science no longer thematizes sensible life or life in general. This nonconsideration of sensible qualities is neither unknown nor gratuitous. Sensibility – more precisely, the subjectivity of these sensible qualities – is set aside because truth does not reside in them or in the subjectivity that constitutes their essence, *because truth is a universal and thereby objective truth.*

This gives rise to the second and stronger meaning of the elimination of life. What motivates this setting aside and underlies it is nothing less than an implicit but fundamental presupposition. It is the belief that the truth is foreign to the ontological sphere of living subjectivity and instead belongs to objectivity in a primary and exclusive way. The same goes for being itself: being is shown to us in the milieu of the visibility of the world. It is what is there as what is there before us. It is what the theoretical regard, developing its procedures and its own powers, will recognize as *what is truly there in front of it*, beyond its subjective, illusory, and changing appearances.

This fundamental presupposition of science does not truly differ from classical thought; instead, it is identical to it and simply extends it. This presupposition has two aspects, positive and negative. Positively, it refers to an actual being, the being that is there in front of us, the being of nature (or at least, what nature is believed to be). It also refers to a truth: the truth of this being, that is, the fact that it stands there in front of us and *is shown*. Even though science, like classical philosophy, may be critical of appearances, it is based on appearances in the end. It just happens to be the case that this appearance is no longer a sensible appearance; instead, it has been replaced by the appearance of geometrical or mathematical being. This appearance still exists nonetheless, as an appearance in a world and finally as the appearance of this world. Moreover, one can say that science neglects *this appearance as such*. Science takes it as an obvious or trivial fact, whereas philosophy turns it into a problem.

Negatively, the presupposition of science – and likewise of the philosophy that reduces subjectivity to an intentional consciousness of the world and, in this way, reduces phenomenality to the world in its worldhood – is that there is nothing other than external being and that the truth is this exteriority as such. In the perspective and language of the scientist, it is "objectivity." If life is the original auto-affection that knows nothing about Ek-stasis, if it is essentialized as a radical interiority which touches all points of its being and which it feels and experiences itself without distance, without the mediation of any separation, any front or any world, then in the words of a science that only knows objectivities it must be said that this absolute interiority, life itself, does not exist. To be sure, science itself does not formulate this explicit negation of the inner essence of life, because it does not even have an idea about it and because life never actually appears where its regard is directed. Nonetheless, its daily work implies the practical negation of subjectivity. This takes place not only in its opening to the world as a transcendental condition of science, but first of all and more essentially, as the radical interiority that defines our original Individuality as a living Individual.

The situation of science in modern culture, or better, of modern culture as scientific culture, is thus revealed to us as a paradox. On the one hand, science is a mode of life that belongs to absolute subjectivity. On the other hand, each of the operations of scientific subjectivity is carried out through the putting out of play of this subjectivity, so that it can focus on the being that is there in front and that is taken as the only "real" and "true" being. It sets aside and rejects into nothingness everything that is not itself. It does not just misunderstand this essence of life – it denies it. It is thus a form of life that is turned against life, refusing any value to life and contesting its own existence. *A life that denies itself, the self-negation of life: that is the crucial event that guides modern culture as a scientific culture.*

The self-negation of life is not only the basis of scientific "culture." It is posited as the sole form of culture. It thereby discredits traditional forms that developed the absolute life and explicitly aimed for such development. The decisive trait of "modern culture" is thus not only scientific culture; it is the elimination sought and prescribed by it of all other spiritual models. In order to have had this enormous and determined effect on the history of human thought, the movement by which thought turned against its past and repudiated everything higher that was brought to it – the self-negation of life – appears as the crucial event. Still unknown as a deliberate and systematic theoretical enterprise, it is what plunged modernity into its distressful situation. This is what needs to be scrutinized more.

First, let us note that the self-negation of life does not refer back to an abstract proposition, a general principle of analysis, or a working hypothesis that is capable of shedding light on a group of phenomena that have their own specificity and teleology. It is instead a concrete process, immanent to each phase of scientific activity. Not considering a sensible quality as such is to imply that it does not count and that it does not have a value of being or a truth value on its own. This is because its own nature – the fact of being felt and thus subjectivity as such – does not count either. This thesis is present and active in each operation of science, in each one of its sense-bestowals; it is what moves and determines its scientificity. One cannot any longer simply affirm, as we did up to now, that by thematizing natural being through the means of mathematical idealization, Galilean science no longer thematizes sensible being or life as a result. This separation is not a mere consequence situated outside of the life of the scientist; it inhabits this life; it mobilizes it and turns it into what it is and what it wants. We are beginning to understand better *that the negation of life is precisely a mode of this life*. This means that this negation is experienced as such. It is not a pure forgetting but a deliberate intention, the *scientific intentio*.

A mode of life that turns against life, that is to say against itself, is a contradiction. Modern science, Galilean science, is this contradiction. We can make it manifest if we cease to consider science on its own, as one usually does, and reduce it to its thematic, objective content. Instead, we have to take a look at the one who is devoted to it, or to put it better, who makes it, that is, the scientist. The scientist lives in the scientific *intentio* that is devoted exclusively to its ideal objectivities, rules and laws, but the scientist exists as a human being nonetheless, in this lifeworld from which theories are abstracted. One lives and goes about one's work, has meals and vacations, has a family and relationships *there*. One is *a living being* who experiences joys and pains, cares and ambitions, even scientific ones.

One is "there" inasmuch as one only has access to what one is concerned about through intuition, that is to say, through a fundamental mode of transcendental subjectivity. One is there "as a living being" to the degree that this intuition – just like all experiences in general only "are" inasmuch as one lives them –is based on the original essence of life within oneself as an auto-affection. The scientist is thus a double person. On the one side, the scientist claims that the individual subjective life, in short his or her own life, is nothing. At any rate, it is nothing but an appearance, an appearance without truth and value. But, on the other side, the scientist continues to live this life that is nothing, eating and drinking, laughing and singing and sleeping with women. Like Tartuffe, he says one thing but does the opposite.

However, as long as it takes the form of an opposition between science and the scientist, the contradiction of science is not an external contradiction, as one might believe. It is not just the scientist who has one foot in the world of physico-mathematical idealities and the other one in this life, which would only be the appearance of the former world, a sort of epiphenomenon whose reality is constituted by molecules and atoms. Science stands in the same duplicity, if it is the case that it is fulfilled as a modality of transcendental life but disregards it and if life provides it not only with the idealities that it thematizes but also constitutes its being. When one contrasts science with this person who is a scientist, one covers over this decisive situation. The "person" is an empirical individual who is presented to us, who is only a part of nature, and who is derived from the same laws and explanations as nature. But if the relation of the empirical individual to science is only an external and contingent relation, the scientist does not construct science as this empirical individual but as a transcendental subjectivity. This is what is concealed under the title of "person" and "scientist." It is only for this reason that they can be conceived as "doing science" and as producing the objects that form its thematic field. In reality, the sense-bestowals of this absolute subjectivity literally "produce" these objects.

The internal contradiction of science as a contradiction of science with itself, however, cannot be limited to the opposition between its objective content and the subjective acts that continually produce it, between what one could call its noematic correlate and its noetic reality. It concerns this noetic reality, first of all. It is on that level that one must measure and evaluate it. What we can see then is an incompatibility between the scientific *intentio* itself – that is to say, the aims of the natural being determined scientifically as the sole really and "truly" existing being, to the exclusion of all other reality and validity, notably the reality of subjectivity – and this subjectivity that is the reality of the scientific *intentio*. So here, in a very rigorous way, we find a conflict exacerbated between a mode of life and its essence, between a subjective modality and the tissue out of which it is made. How is such a contradiction possible? Does it merely result from a distraction of the scientist? Is it because the scientific regard is directed toward the object and its categorical determination, which is itself an object, that it is not concerned about itself and somehow forgets about its own being, before negating it?

But, as we have seen, the negation of living subjectivity – a negation that is the founding act of Galilean science and thus appears as its condition of possibility – is much more than implicit. The elimination of the sensible quality – of sensibility and life – is deliberate because it functions as a methodological postulate. Nothing occurs unconsciously when, at the dawn of modernity and all along its history, it is a matter of modernity building its own image, that of a radical objectivity, a "polar insusceptibility," with complete indifference to the fate of the human being. One must then find *within life itself* the moment and the principle for the choice by which it pronounced its own condemnation, the death sentence of the human being. We can do that once science is understood as a mode of life, as that which experiences itself at each point of its being and knows nothing more about itself. This knowledge does not take the form of an explicit thought or even thought in general, due to the fact that it is a knowledge of life. But if science *knows what it is doing* by putting life out of play, it also knows what it is, as a form and manifestation of life. *The inner contradiction that defines it is a phenomenological contradiction.* It is on the plane of its phenomenality, as an original phenomenality of life, that we can discern its true sense, but what we must seek out first is its own possibility.

The inner contradiction of science as phenomenological and as a way of life turned against life can be understood as follows. A way of life, including the scientific way life as well as any other one, is an experience in the sense of life; it is a manner of feeling and experiencing oneself. The fact that this way of life turns against life means that a way of feeling and experiencing oneself turns against the very fact of feeling and experiencing oneself. Now "turning against" does not initially designate an aim, an intention situated in the ek-stasis of a seeing, a consideration of something on which one would reflect and think, and on which would make either a positive or negative judgment, as in the present case. To turn against life – as a specific way of life, the Galilean way of life – is to experience oneself in such a way that one suffers from being what one is, that is, *one who experiences oneself*. More precisely, one suffers from the fact of experiencing oneself, of being a living being, and of being alive. In the primordial suffering of life, which is the essence of life, and as a modality of this suffering, which is one of its main possibilities, a certain wish arises. The wish of this suffering is to no longer be oneself and for that reason, to no longer be alive. The movement of its self-negation does not occur in life in an enigmatic way; instead, it takes place as its own movement. Instead of abandoning itself to the primal Suffering in suffering and its slow mutation into its opposite, it seems easier to oppose it brutally and to recuse this suffering and, at the same time, the feeling of oneself as a subject and a living being in whom all suffering unfolds.

Thus, the horror of life always results from it and not from an external regard cast on its objective, strange, deformed, or awkward appearance. It is rather within itself, in one of the tonalities by which it necessarily happens and that is like the declensions of its essence, that the crazy idea of no longer experiencing what it experiences, of dismissing its own condition of being alive, is rooted. This Idea is contained in Galilean science, and without it, the project of rejecting living sensibility could never happen. It is rooted in a tonality and extends it as a modality of its development, as the movement in which suffering is trapped in itself and, as suffering, no longer wants to be what it is. For this reason, we ought to say that the science that is based on this Idea rests on a pathos. Ultimately, it is in this way that that it can and must be understood.

The pathos of science is complex. If an analysis of it aims to be exhaustive, it must be pursued on multiple levels. In the first place, the transcendental sense-bestowals that produce scientific idealities are themselves, as acts of absolute subjectivity, affective determinations. They are not simply intentions that open onto their intentional correlate and provide access to it, or, modalities of knowing. Inasmuch as they are auto-affective and inasmuch as no seeing is possible that does not experience its own seeing, these specific intentionalities – those of ideation, conjunction, disjunction, and categorical thought in all its other forms – are tied in each case to a specific pathos. This connection is not just an extrinsic relation, an associative relation derived from the unique psyche of the scientist and his or her personal history; it is an inner necessity. This necessity consists in the fact that such a pathos is no more or less than the very being of each intentionality that is constitutive of science.

Thus, for example, there is a specific joy to scientific discovery, a joy that belongs to seeing as such. According to the modalities, refinement and perfecting of this seeing, it is modalized and runs through the series of intellectual pleasures that are deposited at the basis of the mind as its original phenomenological potential. They are its innate ideas in a certain sense. Likewise, someone might follow the advice of Malebranche and try to make a circle in which all the rays are not equal. In so doing, one will run up against an impossibility. This intellectual necessity leads one to experience the pathos of a fact that constrains it. There is thus a pathos of being constrained by evidence. This does not simply motivate in a tacit way the choice that mathematicians have made in life. In truth, it coincides with mathematical activity itself. It is a feeling experienced in front of what is given in such a way that it cannot be otherwise, the feeling of apodicticity.

Let us note in passing that it would be a horrible mistake – even if this is an error of traditional philosophy and later shared by Husserl himself – to imagine that in order for a feeling to be presented with certitude, it would depend on being given in the evidence of what cannot be otherwise, in an apodictic evidence. What in fact makes it into a feeling is that it is not and cannot be given in this way. It never does reveal itself in evidence, that is, in the ek-stasis of a seeing. For this reason, it is never and cannot ever be the stable and permanent given – what could not be otherwise – of this seeing. It will not be found to be the same in its identity with itself each time that one casts a regard onto it. It will not go through time in this identity with itself, defying change and death. For, the being which is stable and permanent and as such "real" and "true" – the only real and true being – is mathematical being. This ideality, with its atemporal characteristics, is what classical thought took to be an eternal truth and what Galileo took to be the true being of nature.

But this true and stable being, which is always identical to itself and thus considered to be real, is not actually real but only ideal. It does not exist on its own but is a product. It is the product of something that is never there in the ek-stasis of a seeing but, as the auto-affection of this ek-stasis, it is the form of feeling and of life. In this form, it shows itself to be variable from one individual to another. It does not merely contravene the "truth" that everyone agrees about in its universality and "objectivity"; it slips away from it. Through its birthplace and its type of growth, it never develops in the Outside where thought – scientific though in particular – seeks and finds all that it finds. Never being out there in front, it does not exist in the same manner as what is there, stable and permanent, and given to the continual reiteration of an intentional aim.

The original being of life and science itself as a mode of life and a pathos could be described as a static being. *It happens as the continual arrival of life into oneself, as a continual feeling and experiencing of oneself, and as something that is always experienced in this way and thus changes in the same way as the primal Suffering that is the possibility of all experience.* It changes in a perpetual oscillation between suffering and joy. But Life is this oscillation or permanent change; it is willed and required by its own essence, the essence of the absolute. It is not a lesser being but the being of this absolute. It is the sole way for it "to be," that is to say, to happen as life coming into oneself through the pathetic modalities in which it is always experienced and felt.

There are thus two "truths." The contrast is not between the inside of a world and the being-placed-in front that is shown in that way and to which one can always return in order to find it the same with each of these "returns" – to the mathematical ideality that has replaced the sensible given – more radically, it is contrasted with what is outside of this world and outside the transcendental exteriority in which it ek-sists, a more ancient truth whose phenomenological substance is affectivity. This truth is situated in subjectivity and is identical to it. The truth of being-there as being-there escapes from the singularity of the regard that is placed on it, and its pathos vanishes into the Night. Whereas objective and scientific truth is independent from the individual subjectivity of the individual and is defined by this independence, the more original truth about which we are speaking is identified with absolute subjectivity. This truth changes with life. It has *a history*, which is the history of the absolute and its embrace of itself through the fundamental modalities of Suffering. It is an *individuality*, inasmuch as the essence of its pathos is ipseity. It thus only becomes historical in an individual. Its own being is *a singularity*, inasmuch as every pathetic determination is invincibly this one and not another one.

This truth is the truth of the Individual, and this means that it cannot be found outside of oneself and independently from oneself, as being there before it and without it. It can only occur if one becomes this truth. And one can only become this truth, if it takes place within oneself as one of one's own phenomenological potentialities, as something that one can become through a self-transformation and modification of one's life. The "Truth" is thus not initially something in front of which one must disappear, in order to allow being to be as it is in itself. Instead, one must give assistance to it, *give the gift of one's own flesh*, because every essential truth can only occur as this flesh of the Individual and as one's own life.

The truth, as is well-known, is its own criterion for itself. This criterion is the phenomenality out of which it is made and of which it consists. It is the pathetic phenomenality of absolute subjectivity, that is, life itself as identical to and constituting this original phenomenality. As such, this truth testifies to itself. In and through its auto-affection, it is invincibly what it is and cannot be challenged. Given that truth is its own criterion, its one and only criterion is the Individual. It is invincibly what it is in and through its auto-affection. That is to say that it is based on the ipseity within it and essentialized as a Monad and Individual.

The original truth is historical in a mind and body as the flesh of the Individual and because this truth alone matters – the truth that is its own criterion and expresses what it is on its own goes without any "interpretation" and, *a fortiori*, any discussion – and this marks the beginning of what Nietzsche calls "the great hunt." This is the hunt for all the inner experiences of humanity and all the truths that can be demonstrated and tested in life, as a modality of this life and that can be proved to the extent that it will provide this proof. This is what differentiates experimentation in life from what usually goes by this name: the experimentation of knowledge or science. The latter is only the manipulation of an object, the convocation of some process used on its own. As a mere spectator, the scientist seeks to show it as a foreign "truth," the truth of nature. Its alterity, that is its objectivity, is preserved by not intervening in it at all, or if that is not possible, by neutralizing one's intervention and by treating it as an objective process. The former, experimentation in life, has no other recourse and certainly no other aim than to call on the Individual as a giver who gives no less than oneself, who risks oneself, and who will make the truth one's own fate, precisely, one's own life.

Culture is the great hunt in which life gives itself to the truth so that it can be the place of its arrival, its only manifestation and its only possible fulfillment. That is, culture is the set of all experiences in the sense of all the experiments through which life leads to the reality of a "presence" in it, in its undeniable phenomenological effectuation. It is all the virtualities, "desires" and "needs" that are contained in it and that express its original nature. Culture never results from a decision, life's decision to carry out certain transformations of itself or certain "experiments" in order to evaluate their effects afterward. Each decision of this kind presupposes the ek-stasis of a seeing, a way of taking a step back, of detaching oneself from reality, and of knowing it so that one can choose the mode of intervention dictated by it and needed to "change" it. This again is to experiment in the technological sense, to operate on oneself like one operates on the world.

But, *no action on feeling is possible, and as a result, no action on life is possible*. If culture is still conceivable as a self-transformation of life and thus as its action on itself, this is in an altogether different sense. In the first place, it is life and not some other process than it, such as an objective process, that acts. This action is not an external action. It is not directed toward the world and does not have an effect on it. It is *an action outside of the world*. In this way, it is an action "on" life, that is to say, in it. Its self-transformation is the actualization of its own possibilities, the actualization of oneself. Such an action – the slow inner transformation of the Individual –does not ever take itself as its own aim, nor does it result from oneself as its "cause." What is its aim? What is its cause? It is to give each of the powers of life license to be carried out according to its own will, that is to say, to grow, since the being of all power and of life itself as the power of all powers, which makes each one of them what it is, is the growth of the self.

This is why each fact of culture is nothing for life other than the experience of oneself and of one's own Basis, to abandon oneself to the higher power that carries each of one's powers to its highest point. This total passivity of every true action, this letting life come into the self as the growth of one's various powers, is experienced in each authentic step of culture. For example, it is experienced in art by the creator of the artwork, as someone who can experience its splendor in his or her own life, as an intensification of pathos.

Science as pathos obeys the law of culture. As the actualization of a cognitive potential of life, it is not only a seeing that becomes ever more perspicacious; it is also a pleasure. What distinguishes it from the traditional manifestations of culture is that it never takes this as its end. It rejects the essence of life and its growth from its thematic, and it takes them to be nothing. The traditional manifestations of culture, by contrast, are nothing but *life letting itself be felt as what it is in all that it can be.*

Science, as we have seen, completely contradicts itself with this negation of the subjective life, since its essence is a specific modality of this life. If we examine more closely this self-negation of the Galilean life on the pathetic plane, then we must say that this life is not only a pleasure of understanding and knowing. When this project takes birth in life, the striving to eliminate life always follows from a secret dissatisfaction. This dissatisfaction is a fact of life, to the extent that it seeks this elimination. It is a dissatisfaction with its place, to the extent that what it seeks to eliminate is itself. We have given the theory behind this dissatisfaction as a dissatisfaction with oneself: it is the desire of suffering to get rid of oneself. Getting rid of oneself or denying oneself, however, is what neither suffering nor life can do. They are nothing but an experiencing of oneself at each point of one's being. As the phenomenological actualization of auto-affection in the primal Suffering and as a radical and insurmountable passivity of life with respect to itself, they are absolutely linked to pathos. This link cannot be disconnected.

To try to break this link is in some way to increase its infrangibility: to experience it even more strongly. *The weakness of life* consists of its desire to flee itself. That is a permanent temptation, but the true weakness – *what makes it a weakness* – is the impossibility to which this project leads: life runs up against an insurmountable failure in its desire to get rid of oneself. The impossibility of breaking the link that joins life to itself, that is to say, the impossibility of escaping its suffering, redoubles this. At the same time, it exasperates the will to escape it and the feeling of its powerlessness, the feeling that one is unable to escape from oneself. That feeling culminates in and is resolved in anxiety.

The extreme development of modern science must be considered as one of the main attempts through which humanity has sought to flee its despair. If life is essentially experiencing oneself and feeling oneself as a pure subjectivity, is it not strange to see the birth of an *intentio* in life that supposedly constitutes knowledge but puts this essence of life out of play? One might say that science seeks to represent nature. To the degree that natural-being does not contain life's experience of itself and is completely foreign to it, is it not with good reason that the Galilean reduction does not consider what is sensible and alive in it? But the being of Nature is only that way – foreign to life – in and through this reduction. As sensible and bodily-ownness (*corps-propriée*), the original nature also has a place in the auto-affection of ek-stasis and thus in the radical immanence of life. The choice to consider Nature only as a "natural being" that is foreign to life already attests to life's desire to deny itself. The intention to know the objective being of nature as it is in itself, independently from the subjectivity that knows it, is suspect, *if there is no objective-being without a subjectivity that posits it in this condition of objectivity*, and if it is the case that natural-being is given as sensible in this objectivity, that is to say, precisely as a necessarily subjective being whose essence is found where every possible sensation is formed and enlarged: in life.

The joy of knowing is thus not as pure as it seems. One must be able to detect in it the primal Suffering from which it receives what enables one to feel oneself and thus to experience joy, and one must also be able to detect this particular suffering to which the Suffering of our time has already been converted: the being that is dissatisfied with itself, seeks to get rid of itself, and despairs over its own being. The best way to flee oneself is to consider the object exclusively and to consider it as a purified object. Everything that would recall life, everything that is sensible and affective, has been excluded, eliminated, disavowed and devalued in the purified object so that one can know a totally objective being, that is to say, a being totally independent from subjectivity. This is the illusion that we have denounced. And that is also the project of Galilean science whose pathos and ultimate condition of possibility has now become clear to us.

The Galilean project, however, is the entire project of modern culture as a scientific culture. This is what makes it, truly speaking, not a culture at all, if a culture is always a culture of life. Instead, it is its negation: the new barbarism, whose specific and triumphant knowledge pays the highest price, the occultation by the human being of its own being.

Modern "culture" does not merely attempt to reduce all forms of knowledge to scientific knowledge and thus all culture to scientific culture. The result of its aberrant project extends the self-negation of life to the world and to whole societies. It allows this self-negation and its underlying pathos to transpire.

In the end, the self-negation of life is carried out in two ways: on the theoretical plane, it occurs with the affirmation that there is no other knowing than scientific knowing, and on the practical plane, it is carried out wherever it realizes the practical negation of life in some way or another.

Science itself is a practical negation of life. This negation is accompanied by a theoretical negation in the form of all the ideologies that return every possible mode of knowledge back to scientific knowledge.

But science is not the only practical negation of life. In its pathetic meaning, it sets aside the scientist's own life and offers the prototype for behavior that leads all of modern "culture" toward barbarism. Science thereby serves as a guiding thread for barbarism's intelligence, and that is how it has been taken in our study. This study must be guided henceforth by a twofold thematic, first seeking an elucidation of the ideologies of barbarism and second an elucidation of its practices.

Note

1 Martin Heidegger, "Science and Reflection," in *The Question Concerning Technology and Other Essays*, trans. William Lovitt (New York: Harper & Row, 1977).

5 THE IDEOLOGIES OF BARBARISM

Under the title – "The Ideologies of Barbarism" – one should include all types of thoughts that are lived and experienced as knowledge of the "real" and "true" being when one is preoccupied exclusively with objective being, that is to say, with what can and must be brought before them through their procedures. They abstract from life, however, from the absolute subjectivity that life is our only real and true being as a transcendental Individual. Such thoughts do not only posit themselves as sciences but as the only possible science, and they can be divided into two groups – those that thematize nature and those that claim to speak about the human being.

As for the sciences of nature, their law is less undeniable than it appears, if it is the case that what is given as an object is already a reduced nature, the Galilean nature of the people of our times. This is in fact what allows us to define both these people and these times. In spite of the green spaces that one tries to safeguard, nature is neither green nor blue; it is not pink with the rising sun or darkened with the approach of night. There the streams do not run on rocks, and rocks do not glisten in the light; the sky is never threatening and the river never serene. That is because there is no place there for colors, for the light that shines, for serenity or threat. What dwells in the colors, threats and joys and what makes them possible, in and through its auto-affection, has been excluded from nature and does not exist there, except as a prior dimension of the illusions that we are. It is called subjectivity, and the decision has been made not to consider it any longer. When human beings are reduced to this illusion and have accepted no longer being anything but an illusion, they no longer relate to nature – like the cold and the heat, the hard and the soft, the pestilent and the beneficial, food and drink – as a part of themselves, as a lifeworld or the Bodily-ownness (*corpspropriée*) nature. Still less do they take it for what it is, as that for which they are themselves the transcendental condition, as sensibility and Bodily-ownness (*Corps-propriant*). Instead, they are only its effects in this nature, the effects of nature reduced to the material correlates which are regarded as the idealizations of mathematical physics.

It is here that a second group of sciences are presented to us, those that have in view the human being and phenomena linked to humans. They will be specified and diversified, according to their own themes, and they will give rise to objects which are called historical, economical, juridical, etc. In spite of their thematic differences, what characterizes all of these objects, in contrast with simple natural phenomena, is that they cannot be defined or conceived apart from humanity and its essential behaviors. Is not the blossoming of the human sciences a characteristic feature of modern culture?

But, the human being has always been the principal theme of its own reflection and thus an object of systematic and constant study. Can the emergence of the human sciences in the twentieth century and their extraordinary development indicate anything else but the following? The consideration of human life – that is to say of subjectivity more or less confusedly interpreted and perceived as a transcendental subjectivity and ultimately as the absolute life of subjectivity –is replaced with the explicit project of acquiring a scientific knowledge of the human being. That is to say that it is objective knowledge in the dual sense that was recognized above – the aim of this objectivity implies putting out of play the subjectivity that defines the essence of the human being. In the case of the natural sciences, this dismissal of subjective life seemed to conform to the demands of the object being studied, inasmuch as Nature was confused with natural being, with what does not feel or experience itself. In the case of the human sciences, instead, the putting out of play of subjectivity means nothing less than the exclusion of what is essential to the human being. The scientific intention is identified again with the Galilean intention, and for the human sciences its immediate result is the disappearance of their object.

It thus becomes possible to understand *a priori* the traits they present with their appearance in modern culture. The foremost of these traits is the withdrawal of their specific content by erasing subjectivity. In principle, however, every investigation is defined by its object and depends on it. In the first place, it implies the emergence of this object by itself and its prior establishment as a phenomenon, and in the second place, the consideration of a science implies that it is turned into its "object," in and through this act of thematization. Between the original phenomenon and the thematic object of science, it is true that a difference emerges. This difference is constituted by the set of presuppositions and decisions that define this science. For example, Galilean science chose to exclude from its investigations the subjective properties of nature in order to only retain geometrical forms, which lend themselves to an ideal and "objective" determination. We have already indicated the meaning of this setting aside of the being-given-to-subjectivity of nature from its Bodily-ownness (*corpsproprié*) and sensible being, and more fundamentally, of the subjectivity where nature finds its original and real being, as the auto-affection of its ek-stasis. Again, this revocation of subjectivity allows geometrical forms to remain, in their apparent autonomy, as the forms of natural beings, so that physics and the sciences linked to it can keep this primary reference to an abstract nature that they take to be the real nature. But, in the case of the human sciences, what does this radical elimination of subjectivity allow to remain in terms of a reference or a possible theme?

In a sense, nothing remains. That is why we said at the outset that these sciences are without an object. If every investigation implies an object or a theme, the lack of an object gives the investigation a very peculiar style, and this is in fact the style presented by the human sciences today. They are fragmented into a proliferation of investigations that are no longer united by a single aim or a single theme. They no longer develop through a hierarchy dictated by this theme. Instead, they are autonomous. The progress of each one is only guided by its acquired results and the possibility of acquiring other results through the use of borrowed methods that are then simply put to the test. To the thematic emptiness that is the truth of this proliferating development, the same uncertainty and the same anarchy is added on the level of method.

Method ultimately merges with science. Just like a science, every method can be defined on the basis of the object that it seeks to elucidate. The object dictates to science the appropriate mode of treatment to be applied to it, and its way of doing this is originally only the mode of its emergence. More elaborate and "precise" methods are most often restrictive methods, and they are used when the investigation turns out to be unable to respond adequately to the object's mode of givenness. This is where the decision that we spoke about is made: through abstraction, science gives up being equal to the full concreteness of the object and its mode of givenness. By defining itself in this way, it proposes the methodological axiom of only retaining in this object what is "given." This is what it considers itself to be able to handle. In the case of Galilean science, these are the idealized forms of nature. For the sciences that make such a decision, we have said that these forms are what remains, and correlatively, so does their method – mathematics – which is the modality of grasping them adequately.

But the human sciences no longer have their own object and no longer have anything to guide them. Nothing dictates an inevitable way of approaching a reality that no longer exists, at least in their eyes. Methodological indeterminacy corresponds to the referential deficiency of these sciences, or better, their ontological void. As a result, they import the methods that define the natural sciences. That is nearly unavoidable, if it is true that these sciences do not know the subjectivity in which the human being lives and which defines its humanity, and if they do not have to ask what would be the appropriate way of treating a reality such as life.

Since a method needs to be defined on the basis of the object to which it is applied, its legitimacy rests on the fact that reality, whether it involves the reality of nature or the human being, is ultimately not separable from the way of approaching it; its original essence is nothing other than this. Intuition thus necessarily leads every relation to nature, even if this intuition abstracts from the contents of sensibility and retains only its pure forms. In an analogous way, the relation to the human being must be guided by the way that the human being initially emerges in phenomenality and is given to us, that is to say, given to oneself, by the essence of absolute subjectivity as life. But when this has been put out of play and the original mode of access to the human being is no longer indicated nor pre-sketched in any way, then, the human sciences are detached from their rootedness in being and freed from every method. They no longer have anything left but to look elsewhere. All of the natural sciences are given to it at once, and there are no other ones. That is why the human sciences are drawn to the image of the natural sciences and mimic their behavior.

The same goes for their object. If reality no longer dictates its mode of approach and defines it, all that is left is to invert their relation, to define objects by the methods, and to create new objects as possible points of application of all these borrowed methods. The object "public opinion" is thus created by the fabrication of polls, that is to say the application of a mathematic and statistical grid to what can only be discovered in it. This is so called "opinion" not in a general and imprecise form but as a sample of thoughts. The understanding of these thoughts is delineated by the content of "question-answer," and their extension is the object of a rigorous count. These "thoughts" have never existed in any mind but only within this grid, and for this reason, the counting of them, as detailed as it may be, has no importance, except for constituting the "object" of a new science: "politology."

How far can the referential deficiency, the ontological indigence, of the human sciences go today? As insignificant, arbitrarily shaped, and "abstract" as the object undergoing mathematical treatment may be, would it only be the trace or shadow of life, if as an object of science it must conserve some relation with the human being and its humanity? Are not the transcendental categories of life and the content that draws its fullness from life present and acting everywhere? Under even the most objective phenomena, does there not lurk something like the "human," human behavior, and human meaning? Has not the moment arrived, then, to reflect further on the term "objective" or "objectivity," which, if it designates natural being as well as its condition, ends up by including everything else within it, life and its auto-affection?

This is carried out independently of and before ek-stasis; it is never constituted by it. But, this fact does not prevent the possibility of representing it in a world, such that, as has been said, this representation is only a mere representation. It does not give us access to the real and living being of life (which alone allows this access as an access to oneself and as a Self) but only to something that matters to it, which signifies it, and "represents" it – like the photo of Pierre that represents Pierre when he is not there. What does this representation of life consist of? It is an objectification, the auto-objectification of life. It is not an objectification in the sense of a real objectification, as if it were life itself that entered into objectivity and thus were brought before oneself, as if it were given to oneself in and through this objectivity. Instead, the self-objectification of life is irreal in the sense that what is posited and brought before oneself is never life itself – which is affected only in oneself – but its empty representation, a meaning, the meaning of the being of life and of being from life. The phenomenological presentation of what is alive and contains the essence of life in an intentional correlate only apprehends an ideal essence; it is the apprehension of the transcendent essence of life. This does not overlap with its originally living essence, that is, the phenomenological actuality of its auto-affection, instead it only presupposes it. Every meaning aiming toward life or referring to it in any way whatsoever is constituted by a borrowing. It is a trait drawn from transcendental life and presupposing it. Such a "borrowing" is nothing but the auto-objectification of life as an irreal meaning.

Though the representation of life is irreal, it nonetheless fills the totality of the world of representation and determines it from beginning to end. The natural being, in this world, is already inseparable from the signification of "life." In its belonging to Nature, it can only ever be sensible or Bodily-ownness (*corpsproprié*). But a sensible quality is the first objectification of life as its irreal objectification: every sensible property as well as every affective or axiological property of things is thus only an ek-static projection of that which, at the very heart of this projection and in spite of it, keeps its own ontological site. That is where the possibility of every sensation, affection and value remains.

But the world is, first and foremost, the world of human beings. The object situated in this world is not initially a natural being; it is a human object, that is, all of the linguistic, psychological, social, and political phenomena, and so forth. The principle of their constitution is not merely located in a transcendental subjectivity, which models their categories on the categories of this subjectivity. It also gives them their concrete cores, because they are nothing other than its objectification in their material as well as formal elements. They are an objectification of the life that extends everything to them and to which they owe everything. These phenomena are the object of the human sciences. From the outset, they give the human sciences a primary and founding reference, though the human sciences claimed to abstract from them, in keeping with the Galilean project.

Let us consider, for example, history. It unfolds in nature but in the original Nature, in an essential sensibility that is Bodily-ownness (*corpspropriée*) and axiologically determined – the nature of days and nights, humidity and dryness, cold and heat, seeds and harvests, flocks, the woods in the forests, etc. The object of history is the human being in its non-Galilean relation to nature – in its historical relation. The historicity of this relation is ultimately the temporality of the world itself, the temporality in which it takes place as a world and becomes worldly. This historicity is the transcendental category without which no historical reality and no history are possible. Human beings can relate to their world in this historicity and in it alone, on the basis for the ek-stasis of time in them. They project themselves toward tasks and ends that are their own.

However, their content – the substance of social activity – cannot be limited to this ek-static relation to the world. Instead of being explained through it, it can be explained on the basis of life. The activity through which life undertakes to satisfy its needs is rooted in life, in the subjectivity of its needs. But, this undertaking of life is not up to one's free choice – no more than one has chosen to be alive or to take on the tasks of life. The laws of history are thus nothing other than the laws of life. Its temporality is not exhausted by the temporality of the world – in the externalization of exteriority in which a world takes place – it ultimately consists of the immanent temporality of life. In and through life, it is the conversion of desire into its satisfaction and of suffering into joy. Whether or not it knows this, history as a science maintains an essential relation to this ontological Basis of original historicity. It carves out its phenomena on this Basis. This Basis gives it laws as well as a sense; it is the sense and secret motivation of all its work. For, what life wants in history, understood as a fundamental discipline of culture, is to rejoin itself beyond the separation of the world and time. What it seeks is to read its own essence, its own history as sought and prescribed by this essence, in the history of those who came before.

When it becomes the objectivism of the human sciences, the objectivism of the Galilean project is thus only an illusion. This illusion is constructed and deconstructed as follows. Whatever the nature of the phenomena that they study and they do so, the human sciences maintain an inescapable relation to what makes human beings human: corporeity, historicity, sociality, mind, and language understood as primitive speech and as the ability to speak. They relate to all the transcendental categories of life that are defined by the essence of life. These are the fundamental modalities through which an experience of the world and oneself occurs. How can this Basis – the Abyss of a radical subjectivity – be a foundation for the objective treatment of human phenomena and for their own objectivity? How can what hides from the light of ek-stasis enter into it, instead, and offer itself there as an ob-ject?

This occurs through the work of a process of objectification that is the self-objectification of life and its atemporal effect. On the one hand, it is transcendental life that objectifies itself. It is the concrete core of every "human" phenomenon, and first of all, of the human being, the empirical individual. Perhaps this objectification perhaps cannot be conceived without some natural determination that serves as its touchstone, the natural body, but it cannot be explained by it or reduced to it. It is not only objectification that is a subjective process or subjectivity in its ek-static structure. Also, what occurs in the Outside of ek-stasis, the "human" content of the human phenomenon, is a simple representation of this transcendental life and thus its irreal double.

Independent from this objectification and reduced to a natural element – to a being that lacks the subjective ability to feel and experience – this content is only an abstract term. It does not resemble a living body, that is, what carries within itself the power to sense the world and relate to it, first and foremost, to sense and experience oneself. The eye, for example, does not see; the hand as a natural and properly "objective" feature does not feel or touch anything, just as the ear does not hear; it is the mind that does this. If, as a part of the objective body, the hand is put against a solid in order to touch it and to feel it, if the eye sees and the ear hears, it is only to the degree that they are always given as the objectification of the transcendental powers of moving and feeling, seeing, hearing and touching. These define the subjective being of the original Body and are appresented with the natural body in order to make it a human body. They contain within themselves the irreal representations of each one of these powers which are replicated in objectivity.

The objective body and the empirical individual are thus the product of a double objectification. They are an objectification of the subjective body in terms of all our powers of feeling, that is, of being transcendentally for a world. First, it is the Archi-Body, that is, the prior possibility of this subjective body to be in itself, to reach into oneself with each one of the powers by which it reaches out to the world, the feeling of oneself and the experiencing of oneself in absolute life. The human fact, the simplest historical fact, is neither intelligible nor even possible, if it does not concern an empirical individual and if it is not itself the product of this double objectification. This is what turns history into the history of living individuals, that is, the history of the powers by which they relate to a world through the multifaceted variety of their projects. But, first of all, they relate to themselves in the primal development of hunger, cold, and desire in which their actions originate. It is really within this primal development that its own essence – growth–occurs and can be recognized. That is why it is also the development of culture.

In spite of its objectivism, the Galilean project inevitably presupposes this prior given of the empirical individual in the human sciences and thus the double objectification in question above. But one does not do science with the empirical. The objectivism of the scientific project implies the establishment of idealities in which the given lends itself to a mathematical treatment. This time, it results in a new given that is nonempirical but objective in a radical sense, as the ideality of the omni-temporal. One can return to this given as often as one wishes. On the basis of these idealities, it is possible to build laws and correlations that also have the characteristic of absolute objectivity. The sum of these correlations and regulations, in the sense of a coherent and systematic totality, will be a scientific theory of the human being.

For instance, if it is a question of suicides, they can be counted. The mere accumulation of these empirical facts that still lack intelligibility is replaced by something of an entirely different kind, a number. A number becomes meaningful, if it can be put into a dependent relation with other numbers and lead an ideal relation to appear between them. To do this, a given society will be divided up into age groups, social categories, etc. They will be counted in terms of these references, and laws will be found. One will then have the elements of a sociological theory of suicide to which one can add historical, economic, and medical complements. Likewise, if it is a question of human sexuality, one will first define a certain number of behaviors, and they will be listed in terms of age, sex, class, and type in order to enumerate the circumstances in which they occurred. One will be able to refine the definition of the types, categories, and conditions, to cross check them, to demonstrate their forms and structures, in short, to arrive at ever more sophisticated, scientific and objective results.

But what can such "results" be? What can they teach us about the essence of sexuality that we don't already know? What can they teach us that is different from the knowledge that one has in oneself inasmuch as one is alive, if it is the case that each one of the ideal determinations in science is related to this prior and presupposed knowledge? Is it not this prior knowledge, so-called vague and indeterminate (it only seems to be this way in the view of the objectivistic project of science), that must be deepened in a philosophical analysis? If we were to understand a single erotic act independently from the questions of knowing when, how, how often, and under what conditions it occurred and independently from the ideal predicates that one seeks to attach to it, would this not be to recognize its essence? For example, would it not be to recognize the relation of the absolutely immanent, absolutely subjective, transcendental life to its incomprehensible objective double, to this body, with its sexual characteristics and its strange configuration? This is incomprehensible for this transcendental life (but not for science which will be able to explain it one day) which is anxious before its body and before the possibility that arises in it. In order to put its anxiety to rest, it gives itself over to the play of objective determinations and to the future that, in the horror of natural being, has become its own. Doesn't the reader of Kierkegaard's *The Concept of Anxiety* know a bit more about sexuality than someone who would have covered all of the past and future scientific treatises on the subject, with their cumbersome statistics, and who would know what percent of young Americans have had a homosexual relationship before a certain age or that "seven percent of French people have made love in the stairwell"?

The ideal predication of the human condition thus only means its gradual impoverishment, which reaches its highest point in mathematical treatment. For the categorical mathematical act is a purely formal act. Its object is any object whatsoever, and one can count anything without this procedure bringing any concrete element into that which is submitted to it. Does the fact of knowing that there have been, in some time, place, and circumstance so many suicides or so many sexual acts committed add anything whatsoever to our understanding of the anxiety or vertigo that surround these "behaviors"? Is it not clear, instead, that every ideal or formal determination has precisely the result of rejecting this anxiety and, more generally, everything that belongs to and defines the concrete experience of such phenomena, that is, their original and insurmountable subjectivity? Moreover, is not this rejection what motivates it and the Galilean project itself, if it is considered not in the actuality of its operation and its explicit thematic but in the secrecy of its *intentio*, as being itself a subjective experi-ence and a desire of life: the denial of life itself?

From a simply methodological point of view, does not the respect for the phenomenon, that is to say of its mode of givenness – anxiety, in this case – impose a definite style and direction on the idealization process through which all science is constituted? Can the point of departure be situated anywhere else than in the phenomenon itself, such that abstrac-tion is based on it and its retained characteristics are the characteristics of the phenomenon? If the transcendental characteristics of absolute life and its essence are not taken in terms of their original existence, as they are lived and experienced in the absoluteness and plenitude of their concrete-ness, can they be represented in ideal essences? However irreal and abstract these representations might be (and likewise essences themselves as ideal essences), their representational contents remain the bearers of properties inherent to and expressing the living modalities of absolute subjectivity. As such, they have nothing to do with the purely formal determinations that result from the categorical activity of counting, collection, combination or the mathematical approach in general, which finds its privileged applica-tion in statistical methods.

Under the apparent rigor of a system of measurement, they hide the complete emptiness of the knowledge that they allow us to acquire. The mathematical framework cast onto phenomena remains external to what they are in themselves, that is, the immediate life of sexuality, crime, or suicide. The mysteries behind them are deeper than ever. It thus can be said that the more the human sciences call on statistics in order to conform to the Galilean model, the less they know what they are talking about. In the extreme, they do not even have any idea about them – apart from a very vague and general pre-understanding that everyone has about the subjects of sexuality, crime, and suicide. This allows them to define their object, although they add nothing to it. They only repeat with vagueness and inde-terminacy each one of the phenomena that they count and try to take into a system of ideal nomenclature.

In the constitution of every science of this kind, a double process is thus at work, and we must recognize its implications. In the former, which marks the passage to representation, the key ontological feature of life – its experience of itself at each point of its being - is already lost and gives way to the separation through which a world arises. The massive adhesion of being to oneself in the radical immanence of its absolute subjectivity and to the ontological determinations that affect this existence in the perfect self-adequation of its pathos – Kafka says, "Grasp the good fortune the ground on which you stand cannot be any bigger than the two feet planted on it"[1] – is replaced by something completely different: distance and the being at a distance in the finitude of the ek-static Dimension where it is shown. There it only ever displays an aspect of its being, which refers back to another aspect in a play of dis-joined aspects that the conscious regard tries to grasp. Guided by them, it is carried away toward the horizons that emerge infinitely in front of it.

When the emptiness of exteriority replaces the plenitude in which life is essentialized within oneself as it is, it is then that the project of knowledge begins, with its choices and its inevitable decisions. This is the second process in the constitution of every science, and it is something offered for our reflection. Along this finite range of transcendent phenomena, it is a matter of designating what must be retained as an essential feature that defines the object of the investigation: the theme of this science. It is only when these characteristics have been circumscribed and placed in a unified relation that one can then try to locate the laws or forms of their arrangement. This occurs before submitting them to the mathematical treatment which is believed to belong to each science. In the case of the object of the human sciences, the objectification of transcendental life through an ideal meaning appresented with the phenomenon makes it into a human phenomenon. As we have shown, this is constitutive of the object in terms of its retained characteristics, even if only in an implicit way – the characteristics of temporality, sensibility, valuing, affectivity, intersubjectivity, etc. *Prior to objectification, those characteristics are tied to transcendental life itself, according to the fundamental rules and hierarchy that belongs to and defines the essence of this life.* In objectification, they are thus regained as empirical properties whose essential connections are no longer apparent. The positive sciences thematize them by chance, for reasons that no longer have their place in essence and no longer overlap with it. They are tied to other preoccupations and other ends, for example, their ability to be submitted to a quantitative or logical treatment, to lend themselves to a type of analysis or to categories already in use in different disciplines. This is what will dictate the conduct and choices of these sciences.

A dual contingency originates from this dual process is sketched out here. Concerning the objectification of life, it is generally a matter of raising the question "why": why this life? Why these modes of fulfillment? Why these corporeal or sexual determinations? Why these purposes or functions? It should be noted that such questions are not even conceivable as long as life remains in itself. There one experiences oneself and coincides with oneself. One is entirely what one is or does, and one never questions oneself. One has no possibilities and no longer projects a horizon of understanding ahead of oneself on the basis of which one would return to oneself in order to ask oneself: What is that? Why these strange characteristics? And first of all, the most curious of all, why the self-experience of life?

Objectification creates the possibility of questioning oneself. Consciousness, knowledge, science, and the host of problems tied to the condition of consciousness are inscribed in the separation of objectification and devoured by it, and for this reason, objectification is never able to truly resolve them. That is how the question "why?" gets no response (as such, it is the impossibility of a response to that which consists only in subjective life, in love, etc.), and one prefers the more modest question of "How?" This "How?" is never the essential "how?" of givenness. The original revelation of it would lead back to life itself, but instead it is the superficial "how?" through which an objective process unfolds. This is not even its real or supposed cause, but its external ins and outs, which are unfounded like it and joined to it by correlations that only have to be recorded. The question "how?" is opened in and through the question "why?," even if in reality it condemns itself from the reality it claims to replace. The uncertainty of all the investigations that carry the indelible stamp of exteriority is due to the fact that they are thrown into exteriority and are deprived *a priori* of the self-certainty of life. This alone could give them a sense, a direction, an "object" and, in this way, the ineluctability of an absolute foundation.

In relation to the human condition taken as a transcendent phenomenon, a second contingency arises. As we have seen, it concerns the definition, the characteristics, and the meaning of methodologies. The mathematical method has the property of being applicable to any object whatsoever, but it is not the one that designates its object. It does not designate itself; it does not carry itself in itself; it is not the persuasion of an omni-revelation to oneself as in the cases of fear, sensation, or desire – as life. It is only a shadow of this, the shadow of absolute transcendental life that is cast on empirical phenomena, contingent knowledge, and all objective knowledge concerning life. Thought this decision, one chooses precisely what will correspond to this shadow in the supposedly objective phenomenon, what one will take to matter for it, to have a meaning for it, and to be representative of what it really is. It is a matter of building the system of ideal equivalences of life, since the empirical, the first double of life, only enters into the sphere of scientificity with the epoch of the sensible and the establishment of idealities that alone can provide adequate knowledge. What we are speaking about here is the contingency of a set of parameters by which the givens of the human phenomenon are conferred an expression that is as objective and scientific as possible, a mathematical expression.

The construction and deconstruction of the Galilean project's objectivist illusion that is applied to the human being can help us to grasp the internal genesis of the "human sciences". They are the construction and deconstruction of these sciences. Deconstruction shows us the construction – but it does this in order to contest its legitimacy in each one of its phases, if it is true that this construction does not take its point of departure in the original phenomenon but in an irreal representation of life, if the subjective characteristics involuntarily retained (the despair of a suicide, the anxiety of corporeity, the fear of death) are no longer understood in the essential order of their transcendental foundation or thematized on their own, if knowledge of them is reduced to an external enumeration and to the highlighting of external relations, and if the choice of the parameters that seek to display them is arbitrary.

The deconstruction of these sciences is thus a critique of them. It shows how their gain of objectivity is illusory, inasmuch as the continual operation of objectification, representation, abstraction, and counting does not offer an approach of the Essential but instead determines its progressive distancing and ultimately its loss. In spite of the accumulation of positive knowledge that prevails in our times, it shows how the human being has never been less understood than now. In face of the emptiness of this increasing abstraction, should we not return to other modes of knowledge in which life is given to itself in its own reality not just as it is but as it becomes, that is, in the self-growth of this self-givenness and thus in the development and exaltation of all its powers? The only possible knowledge is brought about as life's experimentation with itself, as praxis, and these modes of knowledge are nothing other than the traditional modes of culture: art, ethics, and religion.

Or else, if the aberrant project of an objective knowledge of life cannot be set aside altogether, would it not be due to the fact that it is indispensable to life and thus finds its ultimate justification in it? This point can be formulated quickly as follows: in its auto-affection, life "exists" only as ipseity and thus as a transcendental Individual, and this Parousia of Being is continually repeated, and thus each one of these lives (each of these absolute subjectivities) exists in a relation of radical exteriority with all the others. The phenomenal form of this exteriority is the world. In the world, each life is related to others, to itself, and finally to nature as an other in this world. On the basis of the empirical objectification of each life and thanks to the processes of abstraction and idealization that we have spoken about, the human sciences are constructed in parallel to the natural sciences. The objective relation to others and to nature is only the representation of what, as Desire and Need, has its original site and reason in life itself. Both its representation and what is represented by it can be explained on the basis of life. In spite of their objectivity or rather because of it, the human sciences keep an essential and inescapable relation to life within the Galilean project and the eclipse that it brings about.

For example, let's consider one of these sciences which is rooted in a more manifest way than the others in life as a vital necessity. Political economy is characterized by the fact that the true origin of science is shown through it. It appears in two distinct phases. The first one is as old as humanity and co-substantial with its history. It results from the fact that each living being produces, in a praxis united with those of others and thus as co-praxis, the necessary goods for its subsistence. The division of these products between the various producers presupposes the appreciation of what is due to each one, and thus a measure of the value of these goods which represents the amount of work needed to produce them. But work is a modality of life. It takes on this modality when the suffering desire is changed into the effort to satisfy it. It is the implementation of the original Bodily-ownness (*Corpspropriation*) of nature. But, the living work of this living and appropriating body cannot be measured. It is nothing but its own silent experience in the pathos of its suffering. It is a modality of auto-affection where nothing is pro-posed as a possible object of measurement and where no regard can move to take or give this measurement.

The work that determines the value of the goods and allows them to be exchanged will be the representation of this living work – It is the representation of what remains in itself in one's invisible subjectivity, as the phenomenological actualization of the original Bodily-ownness (*Corpspropriation*) and as its living present. The representation of living work thus only produces an irreal and empty meaning, the meaning "work" or "work having produced this object." As a representation of the real living work that has really produced the object, this representation is the objective work that measures its value.

In order to make exchange and distribution possible, this value must be determined and consequently its measure - objective work - must be determined as well. The determination of objective work is twofold: qualitative and quantitative. Qualitatively, work is either easy or difficult, involves an apprenticeship or not, and one is "qualified" or not. This qualitative determination of objective work is only the representation of the real characteristics of living work, an approximate, chance, conventional or contingent representation, inasmuch as it overcomes the gap that separates reality from irreality and inasmuch as it applies a general quality – "difficult" or "qualified" – to something enclosed in the ineffable singularity of its absolute difference. For example, a painful or unbearable activity for an individual who is not gifted will be experienced by someone else as the fortunate development of his powers or abilities. This kind of general and qualitative delineation of objective work does not correspond to any particular real work; it is an average characterization that holds for an average individual, who does not exist either.

The determination of the value of a product, if it is to make exchange possible, can only be quantitative. For, it is only if this value is measurable in a rigorous way that it can be exchanged against every other identical value. The qualitative determination of objective work in terms of its qualitative degrees must thus be superimposed with a quantitative determination. In spite of its mathematical formulation, it too is just as approximate, chance, conventional and contingent as qualitative determination. It is not actually the living and real work that is measured and expressed ideally and rigorously, instead it is only its representative and irreal nonreal double: objective work. Truly speaking, it is not objective work but only the time during which it lasts. It is not the real time of the real duration of real work, a duration that is identical with it. Yet again, it is a representation of this real time: the objective time of the universe, the time of the world and clocks. Likewise, objective work was only the representation of real work in this same world. But the measurement of the objective time that passes between 8 o'clock and noon, between 2 o'clock and 6 o'clock is called "eight hours." This mathematical and objective ideal will be true forever, but this measurement measures nothing. It grasps none of the actual work, the living work of those who work: they stayed for eight hours in the factory or their office, but what did they do there? One might answer: they did this wall or these corrections of proofs, etc. *That, however, is not the work but its objective result, and according to Marx's brilliant intuition, it does not confer a value but receives one.* It receives a value from living work. Or rather, because it disappears into the night of its absolute subjectivity, the principle behind this value will be what has been substituted for it, that is, the objective measure of objective time of the objective work. This mathematical measure determines all the ideal entities of political economy - value, money, capital, profit, industrial, business, or financial interests, with their respective rates-so that they are all placed on the same plane and, in this way, all have the same status, that of ideality and irreality, in its complete difference from life.

The whole of these determinations is the object of political economy in the second phase of its development. Then it is no longer confused with the practical behaviors of human beings spontaneously exchanging their products based on an approximate estimate, and it has become a science. As a science, political economy is the theoretical system of the ideal, objective equivalents which have taken the place of life. They do not take its place in order to know it – this knowledge is actually illusory – but because, from its most primitive stages of activity, life needed these landmarks in order to be able to fulfill itself and, first of all, to subsist. In this case, life needed to exchange the goods that it produced for the sake of survival.

With political economy, the truth of Galilean science applied to the human being - to the truth of "human sciences" in general - strikes us right in the face. This science can only be built through a series of abstractions that start from life. In this process, life is replaced with ideal, objective equivalents that are quantifiable and mathematizable, such that the latter are the objects of science - work as "abstract," "social" work, more precisely as the objective duration of this objective work, value as the representative of this abstract work, and thus as a representation of the representation of real work –and only have a sense through a primary reference to life. On the one hand, they present the theoretical duplication that makes it possible to measure life, in the form of an objective knowledge, even though this type of measurement is illusory. On the other hand, they proceed ontologically from life, if it is the case that the value of an object represents the process of its real production through living work and is only possible as such.

There are thus two critiques of political economy. The first one is still naïve and is situated on the plane of this science. It consists of correcting some of its concepts, for example, the concept of "circulating capital," to the benefit of other more significant ones, or else it attempts to set new parameters in order to acquire what seems to be a more precise approach to the studied phenomena. It never even comes to mind that this ideal approach only concerns the objective representatives of life and never life itself. Only the transcendental regard that carries out the destruction of these sciences in order to display their founding possibility, that is to say, their genesis, can understand that the substitution of life by representatives that are taken to be its equivalents is the initial founding act of political economy as well as the human sciences in general. This is not merely theoretical. It is not limited to showing the construction of the system of economic entities – work, value, etc. – that seem to be equal to life but are offered in objectivity as an ideal mathematical determination. Why does this substitution occur? Why is there a fantastical construction of this irreal double in which life is only "represented" by being lost? That is what the transcendental genesis of political economy secretly helps us to understand. In the original Bodily-ownness (*Corspropriation*) of nature that actualizes itself in a collective praxis, *each life needs* to evaluate and measure its share of work in the work of everyone in order to grasp what part of the global product is owed to it.

When it is carried out in the human sciences to which it gave birth, the Galilean project is ambiguous and obeys very different motivations. Sometimes it is a question of separating from life and of eliminating everything that is "subjective." It is only felt to be a body foreign to the science that is being constituted, as something that survives from another age, the metaphysical age. More than in the natural sciences, the Galilean enterprise can be recognized here as the self-negation of life which carries the despair of our time within it. Other times, however, the methodological separation of life from the construction of economic entities to replace it is only a roundabout way for life to attain its immediate ends and to subsist.

There are thus two readings of political economy. The first integrates it with the general movement of the sciences toward scientificity and toward the exclusive reign of objectivity through increased idealization and mathematization. The "critique of political economy" is the critique of everything that would retain within itself some relation to human beings, life, and individuals. It is the critique of everything that is irreducible to the objective, to objective forms, to "scientific concepts" like "productive forces," "relations of production," etc. This is a reading of traditional Marxism with its scientific and positivistic aim that culminates in structuralism. The second, the "critique of political economy" in the Marxian sense, is no longer a naïve adherence to scientific construction; instead it is really its deconstruction. It sees the whole economy as a simple value for life, as *Ersatz*, because each economic entity only has a meaning in its reference to life, and more essentially, because it proceeds from life at each instant.

Marxism is one of the two great ideologies of the twentieth century. In spite of the schematism of theses that have become both political catechism and State doctrine, it carries within it the defective principles of the Galilean project and leads to their consequences: the depreciation of life, subjectivity, affectivity, individuality and, in a general manner, all the ontological determinations that are its own essence. Reality and truth are thus not found in life but beyond it in another world, in the great transcendent masses of History, Economy, and Society and in the various structures that they take on in succession and that give them a concrete form each time. With the hypostasis of these objective totalities that claim the title of "Being" for themselves, a singular reversal takes place in the order of things. It is not because there are living individuals that there is a History, but because there is a History that these individuals exist. It is in terms of its rhythm and the character of each one of its "periods" that these individuals exist, that they are what they are, that they do what they do, and that they think what they think. It is not the living work of the living individual that produces capital and its principal characteristic: surplus value. Instead, it is the structure of the capitalist regime that entirely determines this individual and his work. Capitalism is precisely a structure, a system. It develops and grows on its own, according to the illusion that is tirelessly denounced by Marx. It is not because there are individuals that labor that there is a class of laborers; it is because there is a class of laborers that there are individuals who labor, etc.

Along with life, the fundamental manifestations of culture are struck at their root. Religion is purely and simply eliminated, and aesthetics is reduced to a social phenomenon. The approach to any genre of work of art– literature, painting, and architecture – is thus not something specific. With the perception of a new form, it is not a question of seeing how it allows for a growth of sensibility. When aesthetic being is no longer taken into consideration, its appearance is explained on the basis of a certain number of historical, social, economic, and linguistic givens. In any case, they are objective givens. As for ethics, its situation is even more singular. A pure objectivism withdraws every assignable location for morality, since only life can be moral or immoral. This can be seen if one considers, for example, a "scientific" sociology. It explains murders, thefts, and rapes through their social conditions. If only to be able to distinguish between them, it retains in these phenomena only the shadow of transcendental life that belongs to *the act of killing, the act of stealing, or the act of raping.* Because it, at the same, time erases this subjectivity that has been reduced to a shadow, it is wary of any axiological approach and moreover unfailingly discards it. Inasmuch as theft and murder can be explained sociologically through their objective conditions, neither the thief nor the murderer are responsible. *They no longer exist on the plane of ethics; they have both ceased to be human.*

To be sure, Marxism does not exclude all morality; it allows it to remain at least in the form of political action. This has its own rules, but it presents a disturbing analogy with the Galilean project when it seeks to reduce ethical interests. For, if History and Society are the only true beings that have self-movement, there is no other salvation for the individual than to blend into these totalities that dominate it and to go beyond oneself in order to coincide with them and their fate. But all life is essentially individual – every fear, desire, joy and love. The surpassing of individuality is not an *Aufhebung* that retains and transfigures it; it is the suppression of individuality. Or rather, since this suppression is impossible and since the ipseity of life is co-substantial with and defines life's essence, the self-negation of the individual signifies the self-negation of life itself. The political intention in its radical meaning rejoins the Galilean project and repeats its absurdity. The self-negation of life is only the will of life to escape itself. It is not by chance that our own times mark the triumph of both science and politics. Behind the refusal of the "subjective" in the search and demand of absolute objectivity, one same suffering remains hidden. They both proceed from and refer to the same secret discontent of the individual.

The contradiction of the objectivist project is that it proceeds from the very same subjectivity that it seeks to eliminate. The most complex expression of this is found in the second great ideology that dominates the twentieth: Freudianism. On the one hand, it is characterized by the decisive affirmation that the basis of the psyche escapes from objectivity and is irreducible to it. It is at least the recognition on the level of the fact of the radical immanence of absolute subjectivity in its ontological heterogeneity from the world of representation and everything that is offered to us in the outside of any exteriority whatsoever. On the other hand, it maintains a scientific presupposition that nothing should exist unless it is objective or objectively determinable. The psychic unconscious, ultimately recognized as affect, is still only the representative of bio-energetic processes and a natural reality. This intentional aim remains a prisoner of representation, and it is reproduced on the level of therapy and conditions it as long as it obeys the designs of this awareness. A similar teleology guides Western thought and serves as a common site of psychoanalysis, science and classical philosophy.

This teleology of light, however, stands opposed to the position of an original unconscious which never submits to it – its name is life. Psychoanalytic practice always verifies the primacy of the unrepresentable that determines representation and awareness. The work of healing subordinates the cognitive progress to the fate of the affect. Revealing the true nature of all concrete intersubjectivity, the relation of the analyst and the analysand is situated or rather plays out as a confrontation of forces immersed in themselves and in the grip of their own pathos. In this way, psychoanalysis dissociates itself from the human sciences and resists the Galilean reduction and its linguistic reduction, in particular. At the very heart of the devastation of humanity by objectivist knowledge and its exorbitant pretenses, it affirms and maintains, even without knowing it, the invincible right of life.

Even more serious than the elimination of life by the Galilean enterprise and by the various sciences in which it proliferates and scatters, however, its consequences for life appear on the plane of life. Although it is separated, as much as possible, from the thematic of objectivist knowledge and from all the procedures and technical behaviors that it engenders, life nonetheless remains where it is and continues to be fulfilled. It just happens to be the case that these modes of fulfillment are no longer integrated in the general project of a culture that takes them as its ends. They are left to themselves instead, without any stimulation or experience. They no longer make use of any grand model to which they can strive to conform as living and growing responses. These modes of realization of life regress toward elementary and crude forms that are always poorer, stereotypical and vulgar, unless they inverse into the monstrous desire of self-negation and self-destruction. What cannot be passed by in silence now are the practices of barbarism.

Note

1   Translator's note: This is a reference to Aphorism 24 in Franz Kafka, *The Zuräu Aphorisms*, trans. Robert Colasso (New York: Schoken Books, 2006).

6 THE PRACTICES OF BARBARISM

I call all the modes of life in which life is carried out in a crude, coarse, and rudimentary way "practices of barbarism". It is uncultivated precisely in contrast with the developed forms of art, rational knowledge, and religion as well as modes of life that are found on all levels of human activity, including basic forms of conduct having to do with food, clothing, shelter, work, love, etc. It is true that one might ask what exactly does "crude form" or "uncultivated" mean, and how is it differentiated from more elevated and refined modalities – and what do "refined" and "elevated" mean?

A decisive advance in this area is already realized by someone who would remark that, in spite of the theoretical difficulty of defining the aforementioned characteristics and in spite of the vagueness and approximation of the terms that refer to them, everyone understands perfectly what is at stake. Everyone, as Marx says, can distinguish between the crude and the cultivated eye – as if this knowledge were not only indifferent to the flow of words and concepts in which one tries to express it but also preceded it in some way. It would owe nothing to them and would neither be explained nor be clarified by them. This type of knowledge is the knowledge of life. It is the knowledge of the subjectivity that knows itself independently from every other kind of approach: linguistic, conceptual or sensible. Because life withdraws from this kind of approach, every intentional aim that is directed toward it finds nothing but imprecise concepts and empty words. But life is deployed where there is nothing to see, understand or feel, and it expands through the absolute experience of its own certainty.

The domain of this primitive and primordial knowledge is the domain of ethics, that is to say, of praxis. It is constituted by all of the modes of individual life. These modes should not be considered as modalities that life takes on in the course of a contingent and chance history, instead they are modes in fact. They are a *habitus* that obeys a typology, or to put it better, a style. These modalities are modes and not mere accidents due to the fact that they are rooted in the essence of life and are always sought and prescribed by it. This enrootedness of the modalities in life, as modes of life, can only help us to understand better the barbarism of our own times as well as barbarism in general. Before going into this in more detail, let us note that ethics is not a separate domain. Instead, as the ensemble of the modes of life, it shows itself to be co-extensive with life and its full development. One might object that ethics cannot be reduced to reality, if it is understood as all of the experiences given to the human being and that morality cannot be confused with the status of morals. If one wants to be able to speak about morality, must it not be the case that the ends of action are not just anything whatsoever but that those ends are taken into consideration and that a will is explicitly directed towards them? The will would be oriented toward values and would receive values whose moral signification must be recognized, in turn.

Many objections can be raised here. The first is that if one defines ethics as a relation of action to ends, norms or values, one has already abandoned the site in which it stands, that is, life itself. In life, there are neither goals nor ends, because the relation to them as an intentional relation does not exist in what does not have in itself any ek-stasis. How, then, could such ends be imposed on life? How could life be able to want them and move toward them, if they were truly foreign and if they were not secretly its own? Anyone who conceives ethics as a normative discipline and thus as a knowledge prior to action that dictates the laws of action will always run up against the irony of Schopenhauer: "An ethics that would seek to shape and correct the will (read: life) is impossible. Doctrines only act on knowledge but knowledge never determines the will itself."[1]

In truth, if ends and norms can be prescribed to life – ends and norms make up the entirety of what might be called theoretical or normative ethics – these ends, norms or values can only come from life itself. Through their help, life seeks to represent what it wants. But, such a representation is only a chance occurrence, marking a pause or hesitation in action. It unfolds in the immediacy of its essential spontaneity, without objective possibilities rising before it and being taken into the framework of a world. So, instead of determining the action of life, ends, norms and values are determined by it. This determination consists in the fact that one experiences oneself constantly and knows oneself at every moment. Life also knows at each instant what must be done and what is suited to it. This knowledge is no different from action. It does not precede it or "determine" it, properly speaking. It is identical to it, as the original know-how of life, as praxis and a living body. Action, as we have seen, is only the actualization of the primitive power of this phenomenological body.

The determination of values on the basis of life can thus be described and broken down as follows. Life confers a value on things - they do not have any value by themselves –inasmuch as they are suited to it and satisfy its desires. But this spontaneous evaluation by life is only possible, in turn, if life experiences itself, even through its most humble needs, as what it is and must be, as an absolute value. The fundamental values have no other content than what is implied in life's first experiences of itself; they are the proper content of this life. The explicit positing of these values for themselves remains exceptional; it is only the auto-affirmation of life as its auto-representation. But this auto-affirmation as an auto-objectification remains secondary in relation to the older auto-affirmation. The latter is based on the movement of life in its continual effort to persevere in its own being and to grow. This movement is the immanent teleology of life, and every possible ethics is rooted in it. This is true not only for the theoretical or normative ethics that represents ends or values, but also for the original ethics, or rather *ethos* itself, that is the set of continually renewed processes in which life carries out its essence. It is this movement that must be deepened in order to better understand not only what the true nature of culture is, what this movement is, but also the origin of the practices of barbarism that proceed from it.

Life's movement of continuing or growing – its *conatus* – is only intelligible in the recollection of the essence of absolute subjectivity. This movement can be explained on the basis of life. Life can only persevere in its being, because it is given to oneself in each point of its being and the auto-affection of its being never ceases. It does not tumble at any moment into nothingness. By pressing on oneself in some way and drawing its being from its feeling of oneself, it continues to exist and to be alive.

Whoever conceives life as a *conatus* represents it in the form of an effort. What this indicates is that the original work of being cannot be brought to understanding on the basis of seeing what it is. This is what comprehension is. The being of subjectivity - that is, the being of its original essence - is not a being in this sense; it is a work and an accomplishment. It consists of the coming into oneself in which subjectivity continually experiences itself and thus grows on its own in the continual experience of the self. The original being is the being of experience in its nurturing form. It is the experience experiencing itself, and in this experience of itself in which it takes hold and expands on its own, it comes into the self. In this way, this coming into oneself of being or its history is the movement of life, the operation of keeping and conserving itself in this experience. It is able to grow on its own and to overflow itself. Effort designates this movement in its irreducibility to the dead tautology of being; it is what makes being as Life a *conatus*.

This effort thus has nothing to do with what one usually designates by this name, with the irruption in the course of life of a specific modality of action under the form of "willing," for example, with the actualization of a bodily subjective potential. From this effort with a beginning and an end, one can say that it is willed, that it is a mode of willing, or even of the fundamental "I Can" that I am. But the movement through which life tirelessly comes into oneself and arrives in the self in the conservation and growth of the self – this movement is not willed. It does not result from any effort; instead it precedes effort and makes it possible. It is the totally and radically passive being with oneself in which Being is given to oneself in order to be what it is in conservation and growth – in order, eventually, to make and effort and act on this prior and pre-given Basis which is always presupposed. Thus the movement of life is an effort without effort. All effort and all abandon is always already given to oneself on the Basis of being-given-to-oneself in the absolute passivity of the radical immanence of life.

The perseverance of Being in itself and its self-growth are not facts that could be appreciated from the exterior. They can only be clarified by grasping their most internal possibility. This is essentially phenomenological. More ancient than the pre-objective dawning of the world and its ek-static emergence, it does not precede them in order to give way to them and change into them. Instead, it remains in itself within the abyssal Night of its subjectivity that no dawn ever dissipates. In and through this undivided Night, however, the history of Being, about which we are speaking, is carried out. It is the immobile operation in which Life embraces itself in the embrace of its conservation and its growth. This embrace is phenomenological, and the most original texture of phenomenality. Its pathos consists of Life's primitive suffering of itself, and it is modalized in terms of the fundamental phenomenological tonalities of suffering and joy. The suffering of life experiences itself and thereby keeps itself and conserves itself. Inasmuch as this Suffering is the coming into oneself, it brings about both a self-growth of what overflows on its own as well as the change of the suffering of conservation into the excess of overflowing.

Inasmuch as this is grasped as the operation of Life and its consequence, what it does is irresistibly affirmed and cannot be challenged: it grows and overflows on its own. This is to be burdened with oneself, in such a way that, this load at the same time grows and does not cease to grow. There is thus a weight of existence. This belongs to existence in principle and is not an empirical characteristic, for example, as the product of some unfavorable circumstance. Instead, it stems from the operation of life; it is a transcendental effect of this operation. The fact that this weight becomes too heavy and that it can be experienced as a weight and as an unbearable weight, is due to the fact that it is impossible for life to undo that with which it has been burdened, that is to say, itself. This impossibility, as we have seen, redoubles the burden and makes it intolerable. The unbearable is thus only the inner essence of life in its phenomenological actualization: it is a "bearing oneself" that can no longer be borne.

This is both the source of all culture as well as its possible reversion into barbarism. Culture is the set of enterprises and practices in which the overflowing of life is expressed. All of them are motivated by the "burden," the "too much" that prepares living subjectivity internally as a force ready to be dispensed and required to act under this burden. This situation – that is, the ontological condition of life – does not merely determine the great projects of culture, for example, the creation of mythologies as a distantiation from original fears and terrors, poetry as a "deliverance," etc. It resides within every need, even the most modest and routine ones. Something is not a burden because it takes on a specific form or because it is tied to some natural need: drinking, eating, or sexual needs. Something is a burden *through its subjectivity which is burdened with itself up to the unbearability of this weight.*

The usual prejudices of Western thought prevent us from understanding clearly what is happening. We cannot conceive the force that arises in one's experience of oneself in subjectivity. At the paroxysm of this experience, it is brought to its release. It can only be understood as a negation of its proper ontological condition of possibility, that is, of its radical immanence. This is what we are saying: this force is externalized; this tension is loosened; this change into an affect gets rid of oneself. Action is always interpreted as an externalization and a real objectification, such that in and through this process, the unbearability of life is placed out in front of it and thus separated from itself for good. It comes to be materially released and "discharged," in the proper sense of the term. Unfortunately, this never actually happens, if it is the case that force and life cannot cease to experience themselves without ceasing to be alive, and as has already been established, the supposed objectification is only a representation.

Only two possibilities are given for life to experience and assume. The first is culture. Action is never the thrusting outside of oneself of the essence of life, that is, of whatever pathos is its pure experience of oneself, for example, the unbearable. Instead, if it retains what it is and what motivates it within itself, then it is carried to the height of this pathos. Its operation has no other end, or better, no other reality, than to be the accomplishment and the reality of this pathos itself, its history. Instead of dismissing our relation to being in affectivity, it actualizes it. They correspond in such a way that the more this relation intensifies, the more the action itself intensifies. *Cultural creations in all domains are the forms of actions that match our pathetic relation to being, are capable of expressing it, of growing with it, and thus of growing it, in turn.* Such creations do not refer to works in any way, the great works of art or culture in general, or even so-called cultural objects. *They are the pathways opening to subjectivity, inasmuch as its own operation carries out one of the essential modes of its pathetic relation to being.* Culture is the ensemble of these open and given pathways.

If we now call "Energy" what occurs in the pathetic relation to being as its phenomenological actualization - as the irrepressible experience of what grows by itself and deals with itself up to excess–we can then see that *all culture is the liberation of energy, and the forms of this culture are the concrete modes of this liberation.* What this liberation is, to be sure, must be understood. To liberate energy does not mean to get rid of it, to provide an opportunity to dispense with it, to gradually decrease it and thereby to exhaust it and make it disappear. The law of life - the law of our transcendental and absolute phenomenological life - is not entropy. The reality of this life has nothing to do with physical reality and cannot be understood on the basis of it. Every scientific model imposed on culture is nonsense.

To liberate energy, instead, means to give it a free reign, to deploy its being, and to let it grow, such that the action of culture has no other end than giving permission to the Energy of growth, that is to say, to being itself: the auto-realization of subjectivity in the actualization of its auto-affection. Concerning the intelligence of this "beneficial" character of this role of culture, we can only bring it forth within ourselves by holding firmly to the concept of culture that has been elaborated, that is, to the interpretation of culture as action and "praxis." It is matter of breaking culture away from the metaphysical regard of representation that reduces it to its "works," instead we must return them to their proper site, that is, to subjectivity. There is a work of art, in its apparent objectivity, each time that the perception of it, which exists in the imagination, ultimately consists of the self-growth of subjectivity and makes it possible. It consists of Energy and is identical to it. In this way, the work of art and works of culture in general are creations in the sense stated above, that is to say, as an operation of subjectivity conforming to its essence and its accomplishment.

But culture cannot be limited to its works. Because its reality is praxis, each determination of praxis is in itself, in its pure subjectivity, a mode of culture, provided that it is a mode of self-growth and a way of liberating energy. Each eye, as we said, wants to see more. Culture exists when this prescription – which is the energy of vision - is followed in this display of what is seen and in the creation of this display. What is now entirely clear to us is that this energy resides in vision as such. That is to say that it resides in its coming into oneself and in its self-growth, in what has been called its will to power – this is precisely its power, the energy of its seeing.

Consequently, this too is clear. Culture cannot be defined by works, the "great works of humanity." Since it does not allow itself to be limited to emerging only as an exception, it can be extended to all of life. It resides in each one of life's needs and is inseparable from them. *That is exactly what makes it a need and what predisposes it to culture*: it is not only the need for something of which one would be deprived, a mere lack, but the need of the self. Here resides the durability of every need, and this is what determines it as a cultural need: its coming into oneself in the self-growth of the absolute subjectivity of life.

An effort takes place within this growth. Inasmuch as we coincide with this growth, it is not external to us or produced independently from us. The coming into oneself of the life in which we are situated and which carries us into ourselves is also the movement by which we carry ourselves into ourselves. As a result, it is what we are and what we do. It is what we are, since this movement constitutes our ipseity. It is what we do, because we are carried by it and come into ourselves to the extent that it comes into ourselves. Our being in it is thus our acting with it. What was never posited by our action or created by it, however, gives us everything that we are and everything we do. It thereby becomes our own action.

This can never be dissociated from the eternal process in which the Absolute comes into oneself and is historicized. This process, as self-growth, is phenomenological through and through; it occurs in suffering and joy. We are carried along by this process and we carry it out ourselves. This fact thrusts us into suffering as well as the phenomenality of growth. Energy is within us just as much as it is in itself. This primitive Suffering is our pathetic relation to being just as much as it is the relation of being to itself. To employ our Energy, we receive this Energy as something that brings about the growth of our being, and this necessarily passes through suffering. This passage is our effort. Situated within the work of being, it is what we carry out, in turn.

Here the characteristic of the process of decline and what makes it possible becomes visible and comprehensible. It unfailingly occurs on the basis of the following source: *barbarism is an unemployed energy*. The two inescapable questions for every meditation on the decline of civilization are: Why does energy remains in this state? And what results from it? Before even pursuing an elaboration of them, one piece of evidence has already emerged, and along with it, the wisdom of the introductory remark borrowed from Joseph de Maistre who said that barbarism is always secondary in relation to a pre-existing form of culture. This is not a historical situation, with a given culture that precedes its reversal into a process of decomposition. It is the original Energy of Being as Life, or insofar as it concerns our life (the life of individuals, groups and consequently societies), the fact that it rests in this history of the Absolute and is carried out in and through it. The *a priori* of barbarism and culture – the *a priori* of all *a prioris*– is the absolute Life in which we are alive.

Why then does this Energy in us remain unemployed? How can growth contravene its own essence and revert to stagnation and regression? How can there be a stopping point somewhere? Growth is carried out as a passage through suffering and effort. Due to its pathos, this is what gets interrupted. It is in suffering, in its phase of suffering, that this stoppage occurs – and with it an inversion. For a stoppage as such is never really possible. It is not a mere stoppage of life and its development, as the entire problematic has established. Barbarism emerges and is unleashed as its self-negation. Before returning one last time to this ultimate circumstance, let us describe how a stoppage takes on this role and let us describe how it can be observed in the world today so we can see that it is never a mere stoppage but already a refusal and inversion of life.

This world is the world of science. Galilean science has separated from itself everything that is subjective and even subjectivity itself. But it is not possible to eliminate life. Life does not simply remain in science as its unthought. It continues to be carried out in its elementary determinations. For each living being, these are the fundamental needs of its organic subjectivity and of subjectivity in general. Because these needs are one's own need, each of these needs, as we have said, is also essentially growth. It is a primitive reaching into oneself. It goes through the experience of suffering so that it can grow in and through this suffering. While this is what really happens in every cultural process, it no longer happens in the world of science.

Every culture has the need to grow. It arranges the world in such a way that, in all its various aspects, it reflects this need. That is, in and only in relation to subjectivity - for example, the seen in its relation with seeing –it puts subjectivity in relation with oneself in growth. Each construction refers to the fundamental need of shelter: each building, each tomb, each stele, each public building, each village, and even entire cities. In a cultural world, they are necessarily organized as the elements that allow life, in each of the human senses and more broadly in each power of subjectivity, to realize its essence. They allow one to see more, to feel more, to love more, to act more, even if it is only through an imaginary exercise of the powers of organic subjectivity - and thereby to realize the essence of subjectivity itself.

If we say that a baroque façade is alive, it is precisely in the sense that it arouses in the spectator's body an awakening of virtual movements that co-constitute its original corporeity and define it. The play on this façade, along the horizontal and vertical axes, of forces that merge or clash, the wild energies coming from the earth, channeled by the pilasters and that stretch toward the sky, multiplying breathtakingly their power under the weight of overhanging cornices that crush them, the forces that radiate out from the center and run up against the angular pillars before flowing back toward it in order to be immobilized in this gripping equilibrium that hangs above it. Borromini was not afraid to bend the façade of the *Church of St. Charles at the Four Fountains* to the wild course of a wave. These motions have their site and possibility nowhere else than in life's embrace of oneself and in the extreme power of this embrace. That is why they are carried out as life, in the heights of its pathos.

Again, it is not only in works of art that this energy is employed. The everyday actions of the cultural world allow the use of this energy and are ultimately motivated by it. Work, for example, has been proposed for centuries as a "discharge of the work force," as Marx says. Through its most difficult and repulsive forms, it has only ultimately been bearable insofar as an exorcism of the unbearable operated tacitly within it. But it could only do that as a living praxis, as an expansion of the powers of organic subjectivity, and thus as the ultimate realization of subjectivity and its Energy.

Imagine a world where there are no longer any churches or temples, where even the most modest and utilitarian edifice is no longer topped by a pediment or flanked or preceded by a colonnade (as in Ephesus). Imagine a world where the organization of work is no longer rooted in organic subjectivity, where work is no longer the actualization of one's powers through the immanent play of their inner disposition, their coming to themselves and thus the "liberation of their energy." Then, instead of this feeling of liberation, a profound malaise comes to affect existence and numb it. Without being able to exhaust its being by reaching its basis in self-growth and in the intoxication of oneself, each need and motion remains only half way to them and locked into a suffering that no longer goes beyond itself into enjoyment. There is a malaise in civilization every time that the energy of life remains unemployed. It remains in this state because the "more" that it is as more of oneself, as the arrival into oneself of absolute subjectivity, it is no longer able to occur. Nothing is offered any longer to the human being, to be seen or done, as an infinite task that is up to the height and measure of its Energy. It is the endless iteration of self-growth of Life in its eternal coming into oneself that is no longer satisfied or answered.

This arrival does not cease, though – nor does its growth or the more that is inherent in it. This creates an extremely tense situation in which the individual struggles. The "more" continues to be produced within oneself through the movement of life that produces itself on its own. But, nothing happens that would allow this energy to be liberated. None of its powers is used in such a way that it is pushed it to its end and made adequate or suitable to the rising of life within oneself.

With regard to unspent energy, one can say that it is repressed. But, what this repression signifies is something that must be made clear. Energy is not put outside of experience, in a world behind the scenes or a night where all cows are black and where anything whatsoever can be said about what is repressed. Instead, energy remains in the repression. It is given to itself and burdened with itself, with a burden that becomes heavier at each moment. It does not change at any moment into the enjoyment of growth, inasmuch as no activity is aroused in the individual that conforms to its own activity. Immobilized within oneself, instead, it is delivered to and reduced to its pure suffering. It is experienced as something unbearable that it cannot withdraw from and cannot flee. This impossibility of fleeing oneself becomes anxiety. At the very heart of its repression, Energy remains intact along with its affect. Unable to bear oneself and changed into anxiety, one aspires to change into anything else.

The path of growth and culture is closed, however, because suffering folds into its own suffering. Energy is no longer invested in the great activities of art or in those of daily life (which require a continual process of enculturation). This energy thus remains unemployed in the sense that was just described above: it is not suppressed by that fact but exacerbated by it. The affect, its irreducible mode of phenomenological presentation, takes the form of a growing malaise. It thus seeks to liberate itself, but this time it does so by following pre-traced paths which provide immediate relief: the loss of pain. The afflux of energy that could not be invested in the highest and most difficult tasks is found intact on the plane where one now seeks to get rid of it. It remains intact, or rather, is increased by all the difference that separates the more from the less. The share of unemployed energy has only increased, and along with it, so has the malaise.

The same situation, henceforth, continually repeats itself. Every retreat back to the coarsest forms of sensing, thinking or acting gives rise to a supplementary flux of free energy, a greater discontent, and an increased need to get rid of it. Investment and fixation thus become more precarious at each moment. Like a current that is too large and rapid, each flux of free energy rises above the conduits and canals, instead of following their mean-derings and irrigating the land. In the end, they overflow and spill over everything. The inability of a civilization to give itself tasks that are equal to its means – the means of Life – entails the release of its uncontrolled energies and, as always, this sluggishness engenders violence.

If one casts an external glance on what can only be understood from the perspective of life, one can distinguish between many different levels of conduct, according to the degree of affective and energetic investment that they imply. Each time that there is a renunciation at the higher level – this could occur for any reason whatsoever, but usually it involves a recoil from effort and its pathos in cases where effort would be required– this entails a falling back of energy to a lower level. The sharp eye of Pierre Janet was able to detect this paradoxical phenomenon. This displacement that ought to signify a diminution and a subsidence of energy instead displays an explosion that gives lower behaviors an excessive, inordinate, and incoherent character. This turns them into excesses.

However, what this brilliant interpretation of the economy of the mind does not yet see clearly must also be indicated. It is not a real fall of energy which renders the development of higher behaviors henceforth impossible and entails their transfer to the plane of lower behaviors where they reappear as an excess. This fall of energy remained unexplained, and so Janet was left with no other recourse than to attribute it to a somatic cause that was not yet understood. At any rate, for him it was necessary to leave the mental sphere and to give up finding an internal principle of intelligibility in it. But, it is the essence of subjectivity itself that is at the origin of this process that we are describing. It is not an incomprehensible lack of energy; instead, it is the growth of life and its excess that, without being assumed by the individual, produces the sequence of transfers and violence. Evil always comes from the Good and is not a principle external to it.

In spite of his admirable studies of neuroses, Janet conceives the hierarchy of levels of conduct as belonging to human nature and even as defining it. There is a pre-eminent faculty – intelligence– and below it are the levels of action, sensibility, and affectivity. It is intelligence that is the criterion or the revealer of energy. Its exhaustion entails the interruption of intellectual activity and its replacement by emotive reactions, and at the extreme, mere reflexes. He observes this in women, infants, and the mentally ill. But this stratification of the mind is unacceptable, not simply because it repeats unfounded presuppositions. It is also unacceptable because, if life is alive and if energy emerges from life, then the history of this energy resides in sensibility as well as intelligence. Its growth though the experience of suffering and its repression in the various forms of unhappiness with oneself are on all levels the conditions of culture. The development of culture, as well as of barbarism, is full-scale; each process affects all of the other modalities of individual and social life one after another.

Along with each fall of energy, however, energy continues to be produced as life itself. Unhappiness, which is how unemployed energy is experienced, increases. In a very obvious way, then, two paths open up before us and show the figures of barbarism. It is not only a question of going back to more elementary and crude behaviors, since neither energy nor affect disappear in this process of regression. They are only carried to a higher degree of tension by it. This fall, in truth, engenders a growing malaise, in the very precise sense of an ever stronger pressure that it exerts over itself. Along with it and as the sole means to bring it to term, a leap outside of oneself occurs. In this flight into exteriority, it is a question of fleeing oneself and thus of getting rid of what one is, of the weight of this malaise and suffering. But, as this flight remains under the hold of its own pathos - that is, the unhappiness from which it proceeds – it does not undo what it wants to flee and is unable to leave it on the side of the road. Instead, it carries it and reproduces it at each step along the way.

There still remains one option: to purely and simply destroy this malaise that one cannot get rid of. Its possibility resides in the experience of oneself and thus in life. Consequently, it is life's own essence that must be suppressed. No less than the flight from oneself, this self-destruction does not arrive at its goal. The act of destroying oneself is only possible on the condition of being actualized in oneself and thus of affirming the essence that it wants to annihilate. As a flight from oneself and likewise as a destruction of the self, life still remains in oneself. This is how it remains in the world from which one seeks to chase it, in the world of science as well as of barbarism.

The world of barbarism can now be recognized for what it is. It maintains life in the heart of its own project to flee itself and to destroy itself. That is why this project is continually renewed, with a type of frenzy that springs from its failure. This frenzy springs from the failure in which it ends but also from the frenzy in which it begins. This pathos accompanies it in each one of its phases, determining the world of barbarism globally, as a sort of *a priori*. Under the stamp of this malaise, it gives barbarism a unique character, one that is more visible today than ever before.

The flight from oneself is the heading under which one can classify almost everything that is happening right before our eyes. This is not in science in itself, which is entirely positive in the knowledge of nature that it defines through its procedures. But, as we have sufficiently insisted, it is the belief that the Galilean science of nature is the only possible knowledge and the only real truth, such that there is no other reality, as true reality, besides the objects of this science. As a result, the human being would only be real under these terms and all knowledge of the human being would only be a mode or a form of this single science. Here an ideology – scientism and positivism – replaces science, but it is through this ideology that the world comes to be grasped as a scientific world.

However, ideology means something more. What matters in effect is not so much the belief that identifies knowledge with science and the reality of the human being with a scientific object, it is the manner in which this belief is so widely held for more than a century. It sets aside all the others, all the products of culture, and reduces them to some kind of inoffensive luxury, to a game and a mirror of illusions. Even more than its content, the reception of scientific and positivist ideology repeats and clarifies it in a singular light. Its extraordinary diffusion among all types of minds, scientists as well as the ignorant, lays bare its unavoidable condition. There is an affinity of this ideology with the spirit of the times or rather they are a shared motion: the flight of the human being far away from its true being, inasmuch as it can no longer bear itself.

That is to say that this flight cannot be carried out only on the plane of ideology but also on the plane of practice. All the practices of barbarism contain this in them as what nurtures them and gives them their striking unity. None of them, however, display this in a more obvious way than television. It might seem paradoxical to speak here, without any introduction, about the media on the same level as science, due to the ignorance and crudeness of television as well as the refined knowledge of science. But, in both cases, the human being ultimately seeks to dismiss itself, its transcendental life. Life remains, in both, in the form of dismissal. In the first place, let us observe that television does not simply belong to the world of technology, and thus of science, because it relies on a "technical procedure." What it shows is the fact that this process has both been invented and put to work. It abstracts from everything that cannot be reduced to its own being and to all of the techniques that made it possible – it is an abstraction of life and its ethics. No one has asked whether it would be "good" or "bad" for the human being, that is, in conformity or not with the self-growth of life, to reduce the human being to the condition of a vacant stare in front of something that moves.

Television takes place in the world of technology. Its principle is the self-development of technology, its autonomy. This means that it is a system and has no need to challenge manifestations like television. This system as such must be called into question. But, as a system, that is precisely what it cannot do. Every regard that would seek to evaluate it would be taken into it. In reality, it would only ever be its own regard, or its own reflection, a reflection of the system on itself. Every critique then arrives too late, if it believes itself capable of judging that for which it is ultimately only an effect, an avatar.

In truth, who would be able to evaluate the system, to take a look at it with a regard whose source is somewhere else, in a radically other place? Who could do this except for life, which is not an objective totality that can be scientifically known and determined, because it is not possible as an objectivity and insurmountably rejects it? But, in turn, who else but the will to negate life claims to reduce life – and notably the individual whose essence is life – to an element of the system that is subjected to its laws and its structure? This project is not for suppressing life material in its factual existence as a being, but to deny the essence of life and deny the transcendental history in which Being comes into oneself outside of and independently from exteriority and from every exterior being. Structuralism in general and in all its various forms – linguistic, economic, political, aesthetic, psychological structuralism, etc. – attempts to eliminate life and the individual; it is nothing but an attempt of life to negate itself and an expression of its discontent. The fact that this negation of life comes from life itself is the contradiction of structuralism. It reduces it to absurdity. Nonetheless, the fact that it has extended and continues to extend its reign in all domains of "thought" attests to its deep affinity with a world that proceeds from the self-negation of life – with the world of technology and of barbarism in general.

It is thus impossible to set aside the question of television under the pretext that it would lead back to the question of the technical system in which it is immersed, if it is the case that this system, like all systems of this kind, is only an appearance and that it maintains a reference to life and finds itself to be tacitly determined by it. As we have shown, an economic system like capitalism only has an illusory autonomy. It is only a pseudo-system to the degree that each one of the economic phenomena that comprise it are in reality produced by subjective work. Their existence is derived from life and only intelligible on the basis of it and its specific properties. Even though the technical-scientific system itself is derived from the elimination of life, this putting out of play is in truth never complete. Material devices retain an anchoring point in the subjective body, while in a more essential way, the system's putting out of play of life still proceeds from life. Applied to the media, this signifies that it cannot be understood on the basis of the equipment that it develops. It can only be understood through its results for life, from the position life adopts through its connection with the media. The question of the media and of television in particular thus undergoes an essential displacement: from the place of the objectivity where its appearance as an instrumental being is exposed with evidence, to the place of its real functioning as a mode of life, as a practice. What then is television as a practice? Unable to remain and to rest in itself, to be self-sufficient and to satisfy itself, through its own activity, it is a behavior in which life throws itself outside of itself in order to get way from itself and to flee itself. If the technical system in general manifests this purpose, it acquires its most extreme form of expression with the media. Television is the truth of technology; it is the practice of barbarism *par excellence.*

Television is a flight through a projection in exteriority. This is what is expressed when one says that it drowns the spectator in a flood of images. But do not art, the plastic arts, literature, and poetry also propose images to us? But, in its subjectivity, the aesthetic image is only the self-growth of subjectivity. It is thus the essence of life in its accomplishment: culture. So the televised image ought to be evaluated in its internal relation with subjective life and as being located in it. It proceeds from boredom. Boredom is the affective disposition in which unemployed energy is revealed to oneself. At each moment in boredom, a force emerges, inflates by itself, and stands ready. It is ready for whatever use one would like to make of it. But what should I do? "I do not know what to do." None of the high paths traced by culture allow this force to be employed, for energy to deploy itself, for life to grow by itself and to fulfill its essence – none of these paths is presented to boredom so that it could unload what is oppressive about inaction by engaging in life by doing and thus by experiencing its suffering.

One can only move along the paths traced by culture, however, if one has already been involved with it for a long time. The operation – whether it is that of the creator, the spectator, or the reader – is then only a continuation of the continual process by which life is cultivated. That is to say that it is entrusted to another process: its eternal coming into oneself in the growth of oneself. What characterizes the temporality of this second process is that it is not ek-static. It is never separated by the distance of a past or a future, but is temporalized in the experience of oneself. In and through this experience, it leans up against oneself and crushes up against the self, without hollowing out any possible distance of recoil. It is pathos and entirely pathos – its temporality is nothing other than the movement of this pathos, that is, the history of the Absolute in the unbroken plenitude and continuity of its suffering and enjoyment. This indefeasible plenitude is Energy. It is the overpowering Presence of life to itself that lets its force be felt at every moment. "At every moment" means that there is never, in one's pure experiencing of oneself, a way for it not to exist; there is never a no longer or a not yet of this force. This experience does not cease and does not temporalize otherwise than in its omni-presence to oneself and as the increase of growth.

It demands its satisfaction and fulfillment "at every moment," which is to say in conformity with this increase. As a pathos, the nonfulfillment of growth is boredom. "I do not know what to do" means that force is there at each moment and involved in one's being, but no practices or pathos offered by culture allow for the pursuit of this involvement. This unfulfilled force must find some way to forget itself, both itself and its pathos. In this flight from oneself, something external comes in front of the regard at each moment and captivates it – the televised image. "At every moment" now means that what is shown in the time of the world and that, in conformity with its law, must disappear right away and be replaced at each moment by something else that is just as inconsistent, irreal, and empty as it. It is inconsistent because the image is no longer here, as in art, in an arrival of force into oneself and thus in the consistency of life, instead it is placed at a distance from oneself. It undoes the coherence of this consistency and expels it into the dispersal and dissemination of the incoherent and absurd. It is irreal because if it were to attain its ends in the project of this expulsion, it is the reality of the affect that would be abolished. The fact that this project does not end and the affect is never discharged from oneself means that boredom remains together with the televised image, as both its condition and its reality. It is empty because what is in front can only be produced in front through a rising of force within itself, as something that would interrupt it, be discharged from itself, as the emptying of this plenitude.

There is a perfect ontological correspondence, or better congruence, between the "at every moment" of force – in which force is given-to-oneself at each point of one's being - and the "at every moment" of the televised image – which is the continual movement of the birth and death of what is there in front and in which "force" must forget and flee itself as a result of the oppressing pressure that it exerts over the self. The unfailing consistency of life's arrival into oneself and thus the eternity of this arrival is echoed by the "news" that determines television and media in general as the place where they move and as the air that they breathe. Before qualifying what is represented, the news is the actuality of the televised image as such. It denotes the fact that a new image continually emerges in which life is constantly turned away from the self and constantly loses itself. The news is this or that. All that matters for it is what is there to be watched, even though it gives way to another being and, in short, collapses into nothingness. But the new being-there is delivered over to the same fate. The news thus gives way in reality to each new thing. It is the movement of giving way, of emerging and disappearing, and life constantly turns away from itself through this movement. It is the movement of a curiosity that is always disappointed and thus always reborn. The movement of television is as follows: "Television, it has to move."

The emergence of the image considered as such - that is to say, concretely - is continually reproduced. It is the sketch of a place outlined and opened in order for something to occupy it that can be lost. This disappearance is the disappearance of something, that is, the liberation of the place in order that another thing can slide into its place. Emergence and disappearance are thus only the continually resumed act of life getting rid of the self. It is only in light of such an act that disappearance can become fully intelligible. It presupposes that the content of the image is of no interest in itself and that it is destined to be replaced by another one. If it were to arouse true attention and have a worth of its own, instead, this would imply that it would remain and that the perception of it would arouse a growth of sensibility and intelligence in the spectator. This would imply that the mind, occupied with this inner work, would latch onto the image. Like the aesthetic image, this image is not swallowed up by being but escapes it; it is immobilized above time, in the omni-temporality of the cultural object that delivers it to contemplation. But, in such a case, life would no longer seek to flee itself in such an image; instead it would be fulfilled by it, that is to say, by itself.

This is prohibited by the "aesthetics" of television, which is actually the negation of all aesthetics. The "live broadcast" is the fact that everything must be taken directly, without elaboration or preparation. The truth, in the end, is reduced to the brutality of the fact, to the instantaneous and thus to disappearance and death. When this is offered as an artistic ideal and when the work is destined to be thrown away like a newspaper, when all that is worthwhile is something what will no longer have any significance tomorrow and thus does not have a significance on its own, it is indeed the basis of this world - self-destruction, the self-negation of life, death – that comes to the surface again and shows its hideous face. Television is a parade of images, and this succession follows a frenetic pace. The machine functions all the time and in all places, and it must multiply channels and the number of sets in each house. In this way, the parade really never ends. This is not due to the machine itself and to its network but to the ontological essence of television and to its perfect adequation to our world. It defines television as a practice and its essence as news.

The news (*actualité*) determines what is actual. Is this not obvious? But, the news does not determine what is actual in a completely immediate way, as one might believe. Is not the actual simply there, now and objectively? What is there now and reverberates across the entire world is in fact this entire world, the totality of events, persons and things. One must choose. But, what guides this choice? The media makes a schedule for the whole of reality. It only retains what corresponds to this schedule – the "hold-up" in the morning, the racetracks at Vincennes, the report of the trifecta, the little phrase of some tidbit about politics, the rise or fall of the dollar and gas, the rise or fall of gold, the interview with the concierge of the closest building to the place where the rape of a young girl was supposed to have taken place, the crossing of the Atlantic by sailboat, the latest stage of the Tour, literature when prizes are awarded and it resembles a race with favorites and outsiders, etc. Taken in the film of their succession or in their juxtaposition on the page of a newspaper, these events present one common character: their incoherence. Considered in isolation, each one of them is summed up as an isolated incident. Neither its ins nor its outs are given with it. To pull the thread of its causality, purpose, meaning, and value would be to think, understand, imagine, and to return life to itself, but it is a matter of eliminating life. Nothing can enter into the news except under the twin conditions of incoherence and superficiality. As a result, the news is insignificant.

Due to this insignificance, what enters into the news makes a vow to leave it; it is only posited in order to be suppressed. Today one deplores the fact that various television productions – reports, films, dramas – are interrupted by advertising spots. They invite the viewer to continually pass from one program to another program which is just as inconsistent as the one that was just left. However, how can one not see that through this perpetual skipping about from image to image in an inconsequential series, the media realizes its essence? The news does not just happen to be incoherent and insignificant; it must be so. The more that television is absurd, the better it fulfills its function.

The media corrupts everything that it touches. If it encounters something important or essential – a work, a person, an Idea – by the very fact of moving it into the news, the media places it at the same time in the inconsistent. By being there for only an instant, the being of the Essential, that is, the growth of life in its own temporality, is no longer possible. There is a censorship by the media. It is not only a political censorship, as usually occurs and can be seen in the more or less hypocritically concealed effort of power to control the media; nor is it only an ideological censorship that gathers the stereotypes of a time and filters everything through them that lays claim to communication and exchange. Even more serious, radical, implacable and ultimately decisive, in this form of censorship everything that is cultural is, through its own nature, is inexorably excluded from being-right-there-in-an-instant. This constitutes a new dimension of being for the media, and it is characteristic of the modern world. We will call this the media world (*existence mediatique*).

Just like the technical world that produces it, the media world cannot be separated from all contact with life. There is nothing outside of this contact. As its initial arrival in the self, life is the condition of being and thus of everything that exists. The ultimate contact with the life of the technical world and the media world is the will of life to flee itself. One can see that the media world results from such a will by the fact that it no longer does anything. It is content just to look. It does not look in the way that the spectator looks at the work or art. Instead, it only looks in the following way: it does nothing; it does not deploy any of the inner powers of life, not even that of looking. There is thus a way of looking without looking and without seeing. It implies as its correlate a media image that is not just "easy" but nil. This nullity finds its expression in the self-disappearance of this image at each instant.

The media attests to its ultimate contact with life in that it is always a representation of life, for example, of someone speaking or the explosive shot from the left winger who launches the ball into the bottom of the net. In this ultimate contact with life, its project is to get rid of oneself, or, at least to do nothing. This is what the media world shows. In *an existence by means of the media*, it is not a matter of living one's own life but that of another: someone else who speaks, acts, punches, undresses or makes love in your place.

The instincts remain undeveloped and in their coarsest manifestation for television viewers – force as violence, love as eroticism, eroticism as pornography. When these instincts are reduced to their simplest expression, they cannot be actualized for the good but only obtain some imaginary derivative. *The media world in general is this imaginary satisfaction.* For these reasons, television finds its fulfillment and its truth in voyeurism. In the "scoop" of the century, we see the collective death of dumb spectators at a football match by bands of hooligans, an assassination in a spectacular wedging in, compression, crushing, stuffing, trampling, and asphyxiation. It is a horrible sight to see life knocked over, walked on, crushed, flattened, and negated! But this negation of life is no different from what occurs each day with the gathering of millions of human beings in front of their screens. The horror of this negation is no different from the horror of the spectacle that was offered for their delight that night. That is the truth of the media world. For an instant, it is their own truth that appears before their hallucinating eyes.

The humanity that is engaged in the media world follows a descending spiral. One after another, the powers of life abandon the various practices of sensing, understanding, and loving that have been discovered and preserved in the sacrificial history of culture. There each gain was paid for at the price of a renunciation and an additional power. Under these conditions, we have not yet given enough attention to a singular event that takes on a dramatic importance. The institution with the task of transmitting and developing culture is defeated in turn – this is the destruction of the University.

Note

1   Arthur Schopenhauer, *The World as Will and Representation*, volume 3, section 36 (Henry's parenthesis added).

7 THE DESTRUCTION OF THE UNIVERSITY

When something is heading toward its end, the cause of its impending death resides either within it or outside it. In the case of the University – the French University will be taken as our exemplary case – the principle of its destruction can be detected both in its own reality and in its surroundings. In both instances, the same principle is at work. This principle acts everywhere in society, and the barbarism that gradually corrupts society entirely makes it impossible to maintain a University that lives up to its own concept.

What is the University? In the sense of its etymology and its historical origin, the University – *universitas* – designates an ideal field that is constituted and defined by the laws that govern it. Because the laws are universal and thus apply everywhere – at least within the domain that they govern – the university is affected, in a visible or hidden way, by a universality that makes it into a homogenous totality. However, doesn't every human organization and every society obey laws? And before being represented in a legislative or juridical code, are these laws not first the laws of life? Concerning these laws, our earlier analyses have shown us that, on the one hand, the laws of life are practical laws which are constitutive of an ethics in its original form as an ethos, an ethics coextensive with life and society in general, and on the other hand, that these laws of life are laws for its conservation and growth. It is in this way that every society is naturally a domain of culture.

Let us be more precise, first of all, about the status of the University in its historical origin. At a given time – around the thirteenth or fourteenth century in the West – the pope, emperor or king made a formal decision. Aware of its consequences, they founded or instituted a university in the following way. In order to make possible the completion of some tasks and the activity of those who were committed to them, they established specific laws that were different from those that held for the rest of society. Universities were thus constituted on a principle of marginality that was deliberate and not simply happenstance or contingent. We can see the misunderstood trace of this marginality even today, when the ordinary authority of the police and law does not extend to the right to enter a university campus without the express invitation of a dean or a president who speaks on behalf of the institution of the university.

Due to this marginality, it follows that the concept of the University contains a contradiction. If it is the case that what it promotes is a limited and exceptional universality, then this would seem to be a logical monstrosity. But this contradiction immediately raises a question: why are these rules and regulations different from those that govern society in general? Why must this paradoxical universality of the University be instituted? This seemingly abstract question takes on an absolutely concrete meaning, once it is recalled that society as such, as a general essence, does not exist and that the laws of society are in reality the laws of life, the laws of its conservation and its growth. But life, in turn, does not exist as a concept or a general being, inasmuch as it experiences itself and only "exists" as this experience of itself. It always exists in the form of a Self, as the actualization of this Self and as an actual experience of life that takes place. There is thus no History or Society but only "living individuals" whose fate is that of the Absolute. As absolute subjectivity, this only occurs through the indefinite multiplicity of monads which constitute the only foundation of life.

As for our problem, the situation evoked above can be expressed as follows. Individuals perform activities through which they produce the goods necessary for their survival. The forms of these activities are typical to each period and branch of production. Individuals are the site of experiences, but in order for the experiences of a Self to exist, they are nonetheless supposed to present some common features: the "laws of society" are the typical forms of this activity, with all of their theoretical, ideological, and juridical representations. Once again, in and through representation, it is possible to develop a general nomenclature of social praxis, although its essence remains unrepresentable and monadic. Here it is also necessary to speak about "epochs" – that is to say about a "history" of the typical forms of productive activity – because each monadic life is not simply conservation but also growth. In this way, every activity tends toward the "more" as a "more of oneself," because it is already realized on the plane of material life through the production of material goods. This activity is characterized as "progress," a transformation that is at least a virtual self-transformation. In other words, this is what makes it a culture.

However, regardless of whether or not this "more" actually occurs and whether it is properly speaking a culture or a phase of regression, it is a general law of every society that only part of the activities of its praxis obeys the typical forms that, as we have said, define the social work of the economy. Because these activities are the activities of actual individuals, their history is not initially the history of society. It is not History, the history of the typical forms of production; it is the history of individuals. It is their history, and it does not begin in the fourteenth or twentieth century but at their birth – meaning, their transcendental birth – that is, the first mute awakening of absolute subjectivity within them. Based on this zero point of the initial Parousia, an extraordinary development takes place. The pure development of life is brought to its proper essence and thereby to the continual process of its conservation and growth. For example, based on the immobile pathos of its original corporeity, the body "awakens" each of its powers through an operation that connects its various constitutive phases and constructs them little by little so that they can be exercised. The same goes for each one of the powers of the soul.[1]

In principle, this type of development seems infinite. It is the putting to work of subjectivity and thus it is double. One part of it is the auto-activation of the pathos in which our being is internally built. This is why there is a culture of feeling – it is not a culture of this or that feeling, such as pleasure, hate, or sadism, but of feeling as such, a feeling of one's own feeling. This increases to the point of what one could call an ontological excess (*ivresse*). Mysticism is the discipline that has in sight the self-experience of feeling in all its possibilities, and as such, it is an essentially practical discipline. But it is necessary to understand why this self-experience is present in every activity of culture. Through auto-affection, every power reaches into oneself, the power of seeing with the eyes as well as the power of knowing through the understanding, the power of imagining as well as remembering. The development of each of these powers thus implies an original auto-affection that makes it possible at each stage of its actualization, growing and deepening in and through it. That is why, as Aristotle ingeniously noted, every activity is accompanied by a pleasure. This is not due to a chance but beneficial association. Instead, every act – the act of seeing, for example – has its real being in pathos and precisely in its own pathos. Every increase of vision, through its repeated exercise, is the exaltation of its pathos. That is, it is a self-development through its own laws and through the fundamental law of the inversion of suffering into joy. Moreover, this law is the innermost law of life. It is the irrepressible and unbearable suffering of a being that is thrown into itself and driven back to itself with a strength like each one of its powers. It gives force to them and requires them to be deployed one after another. It requires sight to see more and, in the continual self-growth of its vision and pathos, it leads sight to its term, to the inflagration of suffering in the extremity of the Basis.

The topic of this brief reminder were the acts and processes as well as the laws that regulate and express them. They constitute the field of the University, by both defining and belonging to it. How do those acts differ from those which are carried out by human beings in their daily lives? How do their laws differ from the ordinary laws of society? They differ in the following way. They do not have any other motivation than the immediate self-motivation of life, that is, the pressure that life constantly exerts over itself in order to deploy its force. This process is thus the process of culture taken in its pure state, and its power of enculturation appears all the more spectacular when it begins at the zero point of Birth. Its dominant feature is progress. This is dependent on apprenticeship, teaching, and in short, education. This begins at birth and is first the business of the parents. But the University takes over and the different types of progress in all domains – both practical and theoretical – made by the pupil and the student are the reflection of this process of the self-development of life, or in other words, they are the same.

That is why we must repeat that this process has its end in oneself, that is, in life. All of the mediations that take place in the University are only apparent: *to be in possession of language, knowledge, technology, and in and through it, teaching; this is never anything but entering into possession of one-self.* The corporeal or intellectual act that occurs each time becomes, in and through this reproduction, the act of someone who "understands." On the other hand, the infinite wealth of the cultural models that are offered today to anyone who has access to them makes it such that this process of repetition has no end. Even for those who are limited to a specific domain, there is always more to learn. There is no reason to leave the University. The acquisition of knowledge is only a condition for the creation of new knowledge, just as the conservation of life is only the conservation of its growth. The purpose of the University, in any case, is clear: to transmit knowledge in teaching and to increase it in research.

In contrast, in society and its content as praxis, the acts in which it is engaged do not have the growth of life in the one who executes them as their immediate end. Instead, it is a matter of adjusting a room, verifying a check, or calculating a pressure. It must conform to a method, and after this method is applied, the action can become work. It can then be recognized and compensated as such. With regard to work, one can say that it presupposes an apprenticeship and thus teaching, one can also say that it remains subjective in itself. But the apprenticeship or teaching that enabled the individual to carry it out are interrupted at the stage of gaining the required qualifications. The individual leaves the University in order to enter into active life, and at this time, this activity undergoes an essential change. It ceases to be taken in an autonomous and continual progress toward perfection and conforms instead to established models. An activity fixed in typical and stereotypical modes is inserted into a material process of production and identified with it. That is social praxis in its opposition to the university and cultural life as such.

At least until the technical age, this social praxis as a whole still had its origin and end in life. It is nothing but the mediations through which life is fulfilled in a given epoch, depending on the norms and possibilities of the time. But, this fulfillment is reduced to its material aspect, to the production and consumption of goods that are immediately useful for corporeal life (food, sex, clothing, shelter, health), whereas the role of the intellectual, aesthetic, and spiritual needs and goods gradually decreases. And that is because, in the world resulting from the Galilean revolution, the development of life and culture gives way to an autonomous technological development, and this development tends to rule the whole process of production, using it and organizing it at its will. As a result, the individual is faced with a transcendence that is increasingly opaque and unintelligible.

Partly, the material process of production is carried out through a set of mediations and in accordance with pre-set modalities of the division of labor that are imposed on it as a totality. It stands before it as a place that is both derisory and predefined. Partly, this sprawling network of imposed activities is no longer the network of life but of technology. When one of these activities becomes, and necessarily so, the activity of an individual who is in charge of it, *one undergoes a passivity in oneself that is no longer the passivity of life vis-à-vis itself, as is the case with need.* One undergoes a passivity with regard to what is the most foreign to oneself, that is, a technological device. This passivity signifies a radical alienation of the individual. One does not become other than oneself as the result of some magical trans-substantiation, instead the activity that takes over the material process of production and ultimately the technological process of the world no longer finds its reason within one's own life.

The University and Society thus stand face to face with one another as two opposed entities. This opposition is no longer the one that prevailed at the outset. The separation of the University, recognized and granted by a temporal power, reflected a difference of functions within an essential community. One single process – the self-realization of life – took on two different forms. On the one side, it was the acquisition of knowledge and apprenticeship through teaching, while on the other side, it concerned economic activity. Because the stable totality that appears under the heading "society at work" is constituted by individuals who become integrated into society as they go along toward adulthood and into its laws at the end of this formation, the acquisition of knowledge and know-how were different from those of their usual and monotonous performance in a job. The University thus had its own tasks and consequently its own norms, rhythms, and regulations, and no one ever thought of challenging their specificity.

Today the opposition between society and the University no longer rests merely on the difference between their functions. Their two essences are not only distinct but heterogeneous, mutually exclusive from the other. They face each other in a battle that can only be a struggle to the death. As we have shown, the decisive feature of the modern world is that life has ceased to be the foundation of society. From the beginning of time, a society of production and consumption drew its substance from the lives of individuals. One might say that this state of affairs persists and could never disappear. Life is inescapable and inexpungible. It is the alpha and the omega of every organization and every human development, because it defines transcendental humanity – feeling, understanding, imagining, acting, and also the suffering and enjoyment without which there is no humanity or human being.

But we are entering into an inhuman world. "Inhuman" does not refer to a value judgment of this world that would come from on high and that would deplore its insensitivity. It also does not mean that society would have lost all relation with the needs of living subjectivity, such as drinking and eating. That would truly be impossible. "Inhuman" refers to the ontological revolution through which the guiding and organizing principle of a society that found its substance in life no longer exists. It is now only a sum of knowledge, processes and procedures that have set aside life so that they can be established and used. Such a situation, which has been described in this work, is the barbarism of our times. In the society that it brings about, there is no longer any place for a University, if, as a place of teaching, apprenticeship and research, it reunites all the processes of self-development and self-fulfillment of life.

The destruction of the University by the technological world takes on two forms. First, it is the abolition of the borderline that, as an indication of their functional differences, had separated the University and society up to now. Second, once this barrier has been taken down, technology emerges at the very heart of the University and annihilates the University as a place of culture. Due to their importance, these two events must be the object of a precise treatment.

The suppression of the specific marginality of the University is an explicit argument whose true meaning is hidden, however, by the ideological motivations to which it claims to adhere. These are twofold: political and professional. From the political point of view, in the name of the egalitarian ideals of democracy one challenges the right of an institution and those who serve it to escape from the common rule and to constitute a separate field, with its own norms and laws. These are denounced as unjustified privileges. If it is a question of the time of work which should in principle be the same for everyone, how can it be tolerated that in higher education, for example, the professors of the faculty have seen, for decades, their service reduced to three or four hours a week for only six months out of the year? How can it be tolerated that the obligations of teachers in high school or the establishments that have replaced them, is also limited to fifteen or twenty hours, with vacations that are also longer than those of other salary workers? Taken to its end, the egalitarian political argument is expressed as follows: university work is intellectual work. Can this type of work be reserved to a privileged caste? "Intellectuals" should also know the pain of corporeal effort, devote themselves to manual labor, spend time in popular communes, and eventually in reform camps.

The second mask worn in the refusal to take into consideration the cultural specificity of the tasks and the condition of the university is the argument of utility. This one is dear to parents. Don't studies serve the purpose of getting a job? Truly speaking, as the development of the potential of individual subjectivity through repeated practice and the transmission of knowledge, teaching helps those who benefit from it to become suited for a certain number of activities, for perfecting their abilities as well as acquiring new ones. It is evident that the more the level of this teaching is raised, the greater are the choices and the number of "outlets" provided. The idea, to the contrary, of limiting knowledge to what will actually be put into practice is both criminal and contradictory. It is contradictory due to the fluctuation of demand in an evolving world and thus to the necessity of constant adaptation. This ability to adapt is a function of one's degree of intelligence as well as the extent of one's mastered knowledge. It is criminal because it signifies the stoppage of the individual's potential development. It is the deliberate reduction of one's being to the condition of a cog in the techno-economic machine.

It should be affirmed here that teaching, at least, must respond to a dual vocation. On the one hand, it is true that it must enable everyone to fulfill a social function and thereby to be able to get a job. On the other hand, however, it is essential to allow one to use all of one's gifts and abilities in order to realize one's own individuality, that is, the essence of humanity in oneself. This second task is the task of culture in its purity. As for the former, if it too is presented as a partial process of enculturation, then it is something that deserves close attention.

Preparing an individual for a job and for entering into society can take on very different senses, depending on whether or not it is a question of a completely economic society obeying an economic or technical teleology. Economic participation, for example, presupposes the actualization of some potentialities of the individual, while it is indifferent to his or her general development. It can even be opposed to it, if it is necessary to have a nonqualified workforce. One can then take the economic end as sufficient and valuable on its own. To construct the University on this basis is to limit its field or vocation terribly, and if this vocation is culture, it is to destroy it.

Technical participation – and we have shown at length how the economic world changes under our eyes into the world of technology – pushes this dialectic to its end. The detour through "hard science" that advanced technologies claim usually only concerns limited domains of economic activity and a limited number of individuals. The majority remain devoted to automatic tasks. The technical aim cannot be set up as a single principle guiding some educational tracks exclusively and more broadly *an autonomous technical teaching*. Let us not forget that it is defined by the putting out of play of the transcendental life that constitutes the humanity of the human being. What we then see repeated within the University are the very same presuppositions of the techno-scientific world. The condition of this repetition is the gradual suppression of the original dividing line between the University and society. "University of the people" or "University of our time," adapted to the world and its demands, it is all the same. It is only after the collapse of the political ideologies that covered it over that the truth of this entire movement becomes apparent: *after its elimination from society, it seeks the expulsion of culture from the University itself.*

Because society is made up of individuals who enter into professional life through successive ranks, the simple maintenance of its activity implies the transmission, from one generation to the next, of the knowledge that makes it possible. This, as we said, is the task of the University. Two questions are then raised: What knowledge is to be transmitted? And how is it to be transmitted? Let's begin with the latter question, because the communication of knowledge obeys a single law that concerns them all. Isn't the pedagogy of this knowledge prior to all the others and doesn't it dictate the adequate mode of their transmission to them? The illusion, however, is to believe that these specific laws of communication are the formal laws of an autonomous domain. Due to this autonomy that is the essence of pedagogy, *teaching thereafter becomes independent from the content taught.* Some notions of pedagogy are even able to change the ignorant into outstanding teachers.

This is precisely what has happened in French universities over the past thirty years. An army of unqualified teachers were recruited in the haste to handle the influx of students that resulted from the generalization of secondary teaching and demographic growth. They came to be tenurable and tenured. Because it was no longer the content of knowledge that mattered, those who had acquired mastery were no longer at home in an institution where the new teachers were just as uncultivated as their students. Professors (*agregés*), qualified teachers (*certifiés*) and other doctors became the object of persecution and great anger: the most eccentric, the least attractive establishments, the most difficult classes were given to them. As always the struggle of the majority, the weak – in this case those who knew nothing – against the strong – those with degrees – was paired with a reversal of values. As a result of this reversal, the values of knowledge no longer mattered in the University and had to give way to other more appropriate values: good will, social meaning, devotion, the love of children, the underprivileged, etc. The reversal of values finds its fulfillment in a political ideology whose true sense it reveals: egalitarianism, the struggle against elitism, etc. Unionists from the SNI or SGEN and Christian socialists who were worried about fitting in with their time – they have all stopped making intellectual effort and culture their ideal. Unhappy demagogues and all kinds of lazy people work together and lend a hand to the administration and political power. In this new situation, they saw an opportunity to pay a flood of unqualified functionaries of national Education at the lowest cost and also to take the place of the University's intellectual power that was definitively lowered.

The extreme point of this nihilistic upsurge and its greatest danger was attained when, in keeping with Nietzsche's prediction, the strong were defeated by the ideology and the resentment of the weak. They lead the parade and spit on the grave of culture. Although they are professors in title, it was university presidents who challenged the title and function of the professor. They advocated their elimination from University councils and the suppression of theses, *that is to say of every qualification norm for higher education.* Truly speaking, it was not a professional category that was challenged when the service tied to being a professor was challenged; the possibility of higher education was challenged. For all higher education results from continued research that culminates in lectures that it takes months or years to prepare. These normally result in the publication of works that construct a good deal of the culture of a country and a time. To augment the service of professors was not only to lash out against eminent people, it was to put an end to higher education and thus to the research vocation of the University. This augmentation of hours – that is in reality the destruction of the University – was called for by university professors themselves or by their strange union (and this happened at the same time as union demands everywhere else called for the reduction of work hours). This is a terrifying fact for anyone who can recognize what hides under the cloak of political demagoguery: the self-destruction of the University is the self-destruction of culture and life.

Considered philosophically, what does the transmission of knowledge consist of? It is the act by which each evidence that constitutes knowledge – its principles, axioms, inferences and its consequences – is repeated and reactualized by someone who makes it into his or her own evidence, understands this knowledge, and thereby acquires it. Such a repetition is twofold: both theoretical and practical. On the one hand, it is the repetition of the evidence that was just in question–a repetition of the act that produces it. On the other hand, it is the repetition of the pathos in which the act of evidence stands; as a cognitive act, it only exists in and through its auto-affection. To be sure, the purely pathetic determinations can be reproduced in the absence of any intentional aim or "knowledge" – for example, in an act of pure love. It is essential to recognize that this original repetition occurs in its autonomous existence as an ontological dimension of radical immanence. It alone allows for an understanding of the transmission of knowledge that is primal but yet foreign to representational and objective knowledge. It necessarily precedes this knowledge. The first exchanges between the mother and infant, the acquisition of bodily movements, apprenticeships in all forms, the phenomena of imitation and intropathy which are at the basis of the individual and social life – these all happen within the intersubjective, affective sphere that puts into play the pathetic modalities of the monads that participate in and rely on them. To take just one example, in psychology the relation of the analyst and the client is a modality of the pathetic intersubjectivity about which we are speaking.

But if one can and must affirm the existence of a properly pathetic repetition – an affect without representation – the reverse is not true. Every theoretical repetition of an act of evidence or knowledge in the ordinary sense of the term is also a pathetic repetition. It is the auto-affection of this act. We call "contemporaneity" the repetition in which every possible transmission and acquisition of any knowledge whatsoever –corporeal, sensible, cognitive, axiological or affective – every theoretical and affective repetition. Anyone who enters into relation with any truth, whether it is that of the Christ on the cross or the laws of arithmetical addition, becomes the contemporary of it in the sense that was just described: he or she becomes this truth, or what makes it possible. The former case is a practical truth, while the latter is a theoretical truth.

We can add that this contemporaneity has its own temporality and omni-temporality. It has an omni-temporality because it is possible to become the contemporary of an event that occurred twenty centuries ago and, *a fortiori*, with any rational or atemporal truth. "To become the contemporary of" means both entering into the process that leads toward what one wants to be contemporary with and the contemporaneity which one reaches at the end of this process. If it is a theoretical truth, its temporality is that of ek-stasis, while if it is the practical truth, then it is a nonekstatic pathos and thus the history of the Absolute.

Concerning the nature of the contemporaneity from which all transmission and acquisition of knowledge draw their possibility and their essence, it follows that it is not reducible to a formal theory or to a system of formal laws whose cognitive content could be separated. In truth, *the acquisition and transmission of knowledge are identical to its concrete phenomenological actualization in repetition.* They are identical to the act that is reproduced by the representational content in the case of theoretical knowledge and to the pathos that is identified with repetition in practical truth, as is the case with aesthetics, ethics and religion. The idea that pedagogy – or as it is called today, "the science of education" – might be constituted in an autonomous discipline is equivocal. It is true that there is an essence of communication, and we just provided an outline of it. *The pure theory of this communication and thus of pedagogy as such is first philosophy.* This shows that the essence of communication is identical with the phenomenological actualization of the knowledge to be communicated, in its noesis and its noema. The thesis that a transmission of knowledge would occur independently from its possession and reactivation in the relation between the teacher and student is absurd. An ignorant pedagogy is a square circle.

Our second question is what knowledge the University ought to transmit in this transmission that consists of the co-repetition by the teacher and the student of the transmitted knowledge. This alone can allow us to circumscribe the tasks of true teaching. The response is contained in one word: culture. That is, the self-realization of life through its self-growth and this growth occurring in terms of all its possibilities.

Two decisive remarks must be made here. The first is simply a reminder. Because culture is the self-fulfillment of life, it is essentially practical. The knowledge that first constitutes it is also practical knowledge, and as we have said, the study of past cultures gives proof of it, in art, ethics, and religion. Ethics by itself is co-extensive with culture, if it is the case that every living act, including the theoretical, is a practical act, a mode of ethos. As such, it is derived from an axiological appreciation. Dance, for example, is an ethical form of walking and an expression of bodily mastery. We have insisted on the importance of art, which is the culture of sensibility. It too permeated past societies. It was not, as it is today, a separate domain reserved for the initiated and snobs. It was a force guiding the consideration of inhabitants, modes of construction, behavior, practices, rituals, and most notably, sacred rituals.

As for religion, how can its importance for the development of peoples, especially the greatest ones, be denied? In Egypt, it entered into daily life and determined all of its economic activities. Going beyond the mere production of "use values," it gave them extraordinary ends. The various positivist critiques, with their radical but simplistic explanations, fall apart once one perceives the rootedness of religion in the essence of life. It is rooted in the fact that life, as an experience of oneself, is never the foundation of its own being. The experience of the sacred is the experience of this ultimate ontological situation, and the anxiety of death – which is also rooted in the feeling of the living being as not being the foundation of itself – provides the counter-argument to it. This is why we see in every culture that the cult of the dead is connected to religion by a system of inviolable relations – and the same goes for ethics. Because ethics is identified with praxis, it draws its values and prescriptions from the essence of life. For example, if life is always presupposed and never posits itself, that is why no living being ever has the right to extinguish it and why murder, rape and theft are prohibited. Art, in turn, also originates in the sacred: every artwork tells about its own birth. Because art is sacred, it withers away when its religious weight disappears. This can be seen in the West with the decline of painting beginning with the eighteenth century up to its renewal in the great "mystic" works of the twentieth century: Kandinsky, Klee, Rothko, just to cite a few prestigious examples.

Our second comment then takes the form of a question: if art, ethics, and religion are the fundamental forms of all culture and are its essential content, what then can a teaching that ignores all three of them mean? *How can a University do without culture?* The modern and "democratic" University claims to adhere to a certain number of values that stand under the following rubrics: objectivity, impartiality and "rigor," in short, "neutrality." But can these values be evoked in the absence of a general theory of values and their basis and in the absence of an ethics that can justify fundamental choices, identify explicit ends, and define behaviors? There are many choices, truly speaking, that have presided and do preside each day over the establishment of programs that decide the respective importance of subjects to teach and the ways of teaching them. But these choices have nothing ethical about them. They are choices outside of ethics, choices against ethics – choices against life. They are choices where no one chooses, choices without choice, with their radicality and their inhuman violence.

Where are such choices made? Where is the place that is foreign to the *universitas* of the University, and prior to its deployment? Galilean space is the space from which life was excluded. It is defined by this exclusion that serves as the condition of all true, objective, rigorous, and impartial knowledge and as the condition of science. The "neutrality" of this knowledge is the neutrality of this space. It is the Galilean presupposition that leads the modern world toward technology. The modern and democratic University that prides itself on its neutrality, its objectivity, is not without presuppositions. It is built in Galilean space and is prepared to reproduce this space within itself. This has two conditions that we have already recognized, but now we can see their deadly meaning better. On the one hand, the traditional separation between the University and the world is abolished. It is then and only then that the University becomes a microcosm. On the other hand, the content of the world of techno-science becomes the content of the University. It conceptualizes and pursues its "scientific" activity of research and teaching by taking it to imply the deliberate and systematic expulsion of all culture.

The a-cultural and microcosmic Galilean University (and likewise, from the point of view of culture, microscopic) was not established all at once. It is the result of a long process whose phases change and reflect the introduction in the West of a new principle. This principle would destroy not only its own culture but all possible culture, as shown by the ravaging of the whole earth and the elimination of all other cultures by technology. At the beginning, the University included two main faculties: philosophy and theology. After the Galilean period, however, the modern sciences come to appear within it. The first academy founded by Louis XIV in 1706 in Montpellier was called "The Academy of Sciences and Letters." The dichotomy is then introduced between these two groups of disciplines and, at its foundation, poses a philosophical problem that we can now give a clear answer to. The "sciences" refer to all of the investigations submitting to the Galilean project and seeking the objective knowledge of natural being stripped of its sensible and subjective properties. In contrast, the "letters" seek out these properties, that is, the transcendental life as such.

History, literature, classical languages, modern languages, and philosophy can indeed speak about this or that. They can never do without at least an implicit but important reference to the mode of appearing of "this" or "that," that is to say, to a subjectivity that is no longer just a useless and cumbersome individual but the "thing itself." That is what it is all about in the end. When history weighs the good and the bad winters, compares the demographic shifts, the yields for each hectare, these so-called objective givens measure the conditions of conservation or growth of life, or those of its death. Under the mask of conceptual or statistical tools, it still remains a story about praxis and its anxiety. Literature has no other intention than to carry out the same type of disclosure of the essence of life, and if it does so by means of aesthetic processes, this is because art, to which it belongs, is the privileged vehicle for this essential relation to life. Such a relation becomes self-aware in philosophy, and this is its theme.

The dichotomy of sciences and letters is thus based on the difference between their objects. That is, there is a radical ontological difference that separates the being that lacks the ability to experience itself and the being that is defined by such a capacity: transcendental subjectivity or, if you will, Being as Life. The *humanitas* of the human being is based on this capacity. Such a distinction between beings and Being highlights the fact that *the sciences never speak about the human being*. Or, this is tantamount to saying that they always speak about the human being *in ways that are other than itself*: as atoms, molecules, neurons, acid chains, biological physiological processes, etc. By contrast, even if it seems confused and even if they do not have a clear consciousness of it, the "letters" construct a real knowledge of the human being in its transcendental humanity.

In the first place, the imperialism of the Galilean principle and the techno-scientific world that it engendered is conveyed visibly in the University through the gradual repression of the literary disciplines to the benefit of the scientific disciplines. In secondary education, the constant changes of programs and hours are all heading in the same direction. The most dramatic change concerns philosophy. Due to the required nine hours per week, it was the fundamental training for sixty or seventy percent of high school seniors. Its average hours have now been reduced, for all students in these classes, to two or three hours per week. We have to make it clear that philosophy is, among other things, a general theory of knowledge. Its elimination by the techno-scientific principle signifies technology's refusal to be submitted to a critique from anything other than itself. This marks its reflux detachment and its totalitarian pretense to constitute the sole type of knowledge. In higher education, the decline of the traditional disciplines of culture is also conveyed in many ways. The most significant of them is the introduction of scientific disciplines into the former faculty of letters. For example, instruction in mathematics is used in order to introduce students to new statistical methods and other methods that are invading the human sciences. As a result, the very idea of reciprocity as conceivable or even necessary – such as a philosophical, ethical or historical education for lawyers, doctors, and even mathematicians – would seem incongruous.

The victory of the Galilean principle is not only shown by the ebb of literary disciplines but also by an internal subversion within each one of them. The motif of this shakeup is general. Every time that there is in any conceivable way, even an absurd way, to determine the ultimate object of research, the transcendental humanity of the human being is replaced, at the end of a fraudulent sliding of which it is unaware, by some substitute that seeks to count in its place. The choice of it, however, depends on its ability to be submitted to objectivistic and specifically mathematical types of methods. If it is a question of literature, for example, linguistic consideration overshadows or leads astray literary analysis. The text or rather language taken in its residual objectivity replaces the imaginary creation where the aesthetic meanings that constitute the work and the literary as such are produced. This overshadowing does not only result from the invasion of its domain by linguistic categories, the different psychoanalytic, sociological, and political "approaches" that proliferate today also have the same effect. To reduce a work to its social meaning, to explain it by the context in which it fits, or even to privilege "realistic" works for which this counter-sense is the easiest to commit – all of these negate literature itself. This negation is inscribed in the programs and other ministerial pamphlets prescribing that the pieces chosen for French literature classes should no longer be novels or poems. Instead, they should be newspaper articles, testimonies, documents related to professional, labor union, athletic, touristic, sexual life, etc. that can one day benefit the student's involvement in the social world.

The same elimination of culture occurs in the study of "languages," which are reduced to their immediate use. Ancient languages are known primarily through literary, philosophical or historical works and thus are loaded with culture, but they are set aside. The study of living languages obeys the same motivations as the study of French literature. It is only hoisted above the linguistic level so that it can then tip over into sociologism. The goal is to familiarize the student with the daily life of a country, considered in its most superficial aspects that are reflected by the vulgarity of the media. The educational value of platitudes and stereotypes written in haste by journalists who need a story prevail over Shakespeare, Dante, Pascal, Goethe, Dostoevsky, or Mandelstam. In the *agrégation* program for English, English literature has become an optional subject.

The triumph of the Galilean disciplines over the fundamental disciplines of culture and the expulsion of their specific content is illustrated best in the case of philosophy. The theme of philosophy is the transcendental human-ity of the human being; it alone is capable of founding a true humanism. The *humanitas* of the human being is subjectivity taken back to the dimen-sion of its radical immanence, to its original and own self-revelation, which is different from the revelation of the world. Philosophy is not life but one of its effects. It is the effect in which living subjectivity is inebriated by one-self and experiences oneself as the absolute. One seeks to know oneself, thus offering oneself as one's own theme. The realization of this task raises considerable problems, and their solution demands the elucidation of the forms of all possible knowledge and ultimately of their common essence, that is, phenomenality as such. By understanding itself as phenomenology, philosophy gives itself the means to fulfill the program handed down by tradition. It leads it to its culmination not only as a transcendental theory of knowledge and science, but of all conceivable forms of experience, their hierarchy, relation and ultimately a theory of life itself.

Clearly, none of these problems can be examined here. It suffices to observe that by putting subjectivity out of play, the Galilean project takes away philosophy's proper object. This putting out of play, which had only a methodological significance for Galileo, that aimed for the nonsubjective knowledge of a being in itself, gets a dogmatic meaning. As with positivism, philosophy is condemned to death. It is not a matter of our concern that this dogmatic elimination of subjectivity, within a problem of knowledge whose essence is subjectivity, is absurd or that it results in a huge contradic-tion for the founder of positivism that prompts a massive return of feeling in the place from which life was just driven away. Let's remain content to observe the lot reserved for philosophy in the neopositivist University.

Alongside the ebb mentioned above and comparable to those of litera-ture, classical languages, art, and culture in general, philosophy is reduced to a reflection on scientific knowledge as the only valid knowledge. It becomes epistemology. Or else, given that science comes to be the authentic reflec-tion of science on itself, it is a mere history of the sciences. At the CNRS (*Centre National de la Recherche Scientifique*), philosophy has the forty-fifth and last section under the heading "Philosophy, Epistemology, History of Science." There is always a discussion of whether to purely and simply elim-inate this section. In the best cases, it becomes *a posteriori* knowledge of the development of a particular type of knowledge in the modern world. That is what has replaced the immense undertaking of elucidating the essence of life and the transcendental humanity of the human being.

At the extreme point of its completion, the dogmatic negation of tran-scendental life does not just pervert philosophy; it eliminates philosophy to the benefit of a new discipline: positive or scientific psychology. Classical philosophy took care of psychology, inasmuch as *psyche* means soul or subjectivity and *logos* is the knowledge of it. Psycho-logy is the definition of philosophy. The radical, ontological negation of subjectivity occurs at the beginning of the twentieth century with the emergence of behaviorism, and its contradictory nature has already been shown. All that remains, after consciousness is eliminated, is to find a new object for this science: this will be behavior. Behavior implies the objectification of a transcendental subjectivity that alone can give it its "sense." That is why scientific psychology can only truly arrive at its goal by challenging the specificity and autonomy of human behavior, by interpreting it as a mere appearance, as the epiphenomenon or result of a process that is biological. With this attempt to produce an exhaustive explication of subjectivity on the basis of biology, "scientific" psychology reveals its most ultimate materialist presupposition. It self-destructs as an autonomous discipline in order to give voice to a science of nature. The alienation of the human being is thus pushed to its extreme limit. Everything that is human is explained through what is in no way human. Scientific and materialist psychology thus appears as the truth of the Galilean project applied to the human being, and it consists of the elimination of its own essence.

But subjectivity can never be explained, even a little bit, if the mental, that is, the shadow it casts on the world, is explained through the biological. And that is because if "A" is biological and "B" is mental, the connection between "A" and "B" escapes. "B" can only ever be ascertained on its own level, *in and through itself*, as something that is absolutely new and irreducible in relation to the biological, or to speak like Descartes, an innate idea.[2] One cannot deduce the knowledge of the mental (of red, pain etc.) on the basis of biological or chemical processes. Instead, one must start from the mental by positing it and presupposing it as it is posited, presupposed and knows itself, in order to ascertain their correlation. This correlation only introduces the representation of subjectivity in the human mind and never subjectivity itself, which withdraws and remains in the nonecstatic Night of its pure immanence.

The fact that one cannot obtain the least knowledge about the subjective by starting from the biological is what must be realized by all thought (whether scientism or materialism) whose practices require a correct understanding of the phenomena in question. Speaking about the deep mind, or what he calls "the latent states of psychic life," Freud states categorically: "These are, at the present time, completely inaccessible to us in their psychic characteristics; no physiological representation or chemical process can provide us with an idea about their nature."[3] If one takes a look at the disciplines placed under the rubric of "psychology" in the University today, one discovers that, alongside the scientific psychology of behavior that points back to biology, there is the teaching of psychoanalysis. But, no theoretical justification is given for this strange juxtaposition of heterogeneous investigations that follow their own paths and do not know anything about one another. The reason for this situation is clear to us: it is the strict consequence of the absurdity of the Galilean project applied to the knowledge of the human being. The expulsion of transcendental life from the domain of knowledge by the objectivist psychology of behavior entails its repression in the "unconscious," and this is what is recovered by psychoanalysis. Psychoanalysis is the unconscious substitute of philosophy and takes up its task once again: the delineation of the *humanitas* of the human being. This recovery is impossible without a transcendental and eidetic method and without a conscious rupture with Galilean objectivism to which, in a contradictory way, psychoanalysis continually returns. That is why it has only been able to build a bastard psychology – half-subjective and half-objective – an empirical psychology in which the attempt to make empirical concepts (relation to the Father, anal sexuality, etc.) play a transcendental role can only result in the most extreme confusion.

As an application of the Galilean project to the knowledge of the human being, psychology presents itself as the prototype of the new "human sciences," and in Chapter 5 we offered a general theory of their deconstruction. The development of a specific teaching of psychology, its attempt to replace philosophy or at least traditional "philosophical psychology," and to present itself as a scientific knowledge of the human being in place of the old metaphysical dreams – all of that attests in a striking way to the continual progress of the Galilean principle within the University and the literary disciplines. Alongside psychology, the emergence of a sociology that follows the same presuppositions and claims the same title of scientificity has the same sense. It is thus in reality a very specific kind of sociology.[4] No more than psychology, a sociology concerned with the humanity of the human being and putting it into play could not do without a transcendental basis, consisting of the intersubjectivity which is at the basis of any social phenomenon whatsoever. On the one hand, the content of this intersubjectivity is nothing but the individual subjectivities that enter into relation, such that its laws, the laws of society, are no different from those of the individuals that compose it. On the other hand, this intersubjectivity must be thought on its own, not simply as a result or a state of affairs. It must be thought of in terms of the transcendental process of its formation, which gives rise to it or through which it gives rise to itself. This task was carried out in the work of a great philosopher, the French sociologist Gabriel Tarde. Through an elucidation of the crucial phenomenon of imitation, Tarde was able to delve deeply into the transcendental process of this self-constitution of concrete intersubjectivity.

But the setting aside of transcendental subjectivity by the Galilean project is also a setting aside of intersubjectivity. Scientific sociology must, just like scientific psychology, give itself another object. Once again, it will replace a subjective essence with "behaviors" or "phenomena" that are reduced to their being-given in the objectivity of society – such behaviors or phenomena are no longer individual but social. Inasmuch as behaviors must be abstracted from intersubjectivity just like the behaviors of psychology were abstracted from subjectivity, it is necessary for them to subsist on their own and not through this subjectivity without which they would have neither content nor sense. In order to found an objectivistic and thus scientific sociology, the decisive point formulated by Durkheim was the hypostasis of society and social processes with, as their correlate, autonomous sociological laws that were independent from the laws of individual subjectivity and moreover imposed on it. The absurdity by which "the life of this society follows laws opposed to the laws that act on the human being as an individual" – an absurdity denounced by Marx in his polemic against Proudhon[5] – became the explicit principle of the new sociology. Conveyed by a Marxism that did not know anything about Marx, it would completely block out Tarde's sociology, and along with it, the possibility of a dynamic and living sociology.

We have shown how this objectivist sociology with a scientific aim is paired with a political ideology and a contestable ethics, in the Marxism that became Leninism. Because the relation between Society and the Individual (which are in reality the Same, which have the same substance – subjectivity, intersubjectivity, praxis – so that their laws are also the same) is conceived as an external causal relation between two separate entities, Society becomes the cause of the Individual. Then, in order to break away from this derisory condition, the individual only has the option to be devoted to political tasks and to be identified in a quasimetaphysical fashion with the fate of the world. We understand the meaning of this flight outside of oneself by life and the individual, and how in reality its source is in them. In spite of their conceptual mediocrity, the sociology built on the ruins of individual life and the human sciences responding to the same aim are only able to obtain their success because, behind the Galilean glitz that they put on, they refer back in each case to despair as the real force by which they secretly are nourished.

This "scientific" sociology takes on a decisive importance for the question of the University. Not content to contribute to the repression of traditional disciplines, it strikes each one of them in the heart. It takes away their own object and their right to speak. Sociologized history is no longer about living individuals but the transcendent structures under which they succumb. The possibility – which made history a form of culture – no longer exists for the historical to acquire a deeper and clearer view of the *humanitas* of the human being or to respond to beings of the past and their highest experiences through repetition. Yet again, the external study of forms and general configurations replaces the penetration into the secret of what each individual really was. We have denounced what the sociological approach implies in literature: the misunderstanding of literature as such. As for philosophy, it is no more than a branch of sociology. It is no longer situated in a universal theory of knowledge, instead by taking its place, *sociological explication turns philosophy into an ideology*, an effect in place of a principle and a foyer of intelligibility. The history of philosophy is no longer anything but the history of ideas, a mere facticity stuck in an empirical totality and only comprehensible on that basis.

Inasmuch as the ideal universe as a whole is a function of society and its prior organization, so too the University, where this world develops and is concretely identified with it, is no longer anything but an effect of this society and its product. The split between Society and the Individual no longer has any rationale after the autonomy of the individual is challenged. Durkheimian and Leninist sociology, with its many offsprings, requires the suppression of this demarcating line, and it undermines, in each of the fundamental disciplines of culture, its right to autonomy. The suppression of this right, or if you will, the hegemony of social states of affairs must be thought of in terms of the three-fold structure of all societies: political, economic, and today techno-scientific. Political subordination means totalitarianism. Economic subordination means the imposition of a foreign goal on every form of activity – notably intellectual and spiritual activities; it implies the reversal of vital teleology. Techno-scientific subordination, with its political and administrative connections, demands the expulsion of culture from the place intended for its development and thus the pure and simple destruction of a University devoted to culture.

A fourth consequence can be added to the three mentioned above, and it is the one that gives modern "democracies" their proper physiognomy. The elimination of transcendental subjectivity by the Galilean project is never complete. Life continues but, as we said, in the coarsest ways: basic instincts are fulfilled without reference to a cultural model or a more demanding sensibility. Force is fulfilled in its most brutal ways; thought is reduced to ideological schemas, to shocking words and the weight of photos, in short, to collective representations that have become a faithful reflection of an existence that skims the surface. The poverty of this social existence is shown in the media, at the same time as it shaped and perverted by the media. When a change of educational curriculum is motivated by political sociologism and requires the replacement of the study of great writers by those of the social environment and the replacement of philosophical texts by audiovisual information, these degraded forms of life come to replace, as mental or even ideal content, the developed and exalted productions of culture.

But everything holds. Culture is self-referential. No major work can be explained in an immediate way. Its genesis implies all of the preceding investigations in a cultural world to which it refers through a complex play of continuities and ruptures. The reactivation of them is indispensable for understanding a work and also gives works an extraordinary ability to open and enrich. It is much easier to prepare a dossier on a question of current events. Unqualified teachers who have never studied the subject they are required to teach, which account for more than 30 percent of teachers according to one report, are sufficient. The elimination of culture and the lowering of the university's standing work in tandem. Under the aegis of sociologism and in the name of preparing students for "social reality," daily banality, ordinary behaviors, rudimentary phantasms, the language of the media or analphabets have become the norm and what is to be taught.

The two questions put to the University concerned the nature of the knowledge to be transmitted and how it was to be transmitted. The change of content that perverts traditional disciplines and replaces them with supposed sciences – which seek to raise the uncertain features of an empirical state up to the rank of theoretical norms – is accompanied by a change in the mode of transmission of teaching as such that is no less essential. Repetition in the productive contemporaneity of apodictic evidence and pathetic certainty is contrasted with the communication of information about facts that are external and superficial and can be assimilated with a pure factuality. Where does this model come from? In a society engendered by the blind self-development of techno-science and its overturning of earlier stratifications, technical devices gradually replace the subjective praxis of human beings. Communication is no longer a living relation based on the personal word and always derived from individuals who enter into relation. It is no longer intersubjectivity but precisely a technical network. It has become media communication and is reducible to it.

The essence of media communication is television. What media communication communicates is itself, in such a way that the form of this communication becomes its content. This is why something can only be real, if and only if it enters into this communication. What matters is the number of journalists, the number of cameras gathered around what will come into being in and through them: the event. In and through them, the event does not only derive its importance but its existence. The media world thus determines its nature. For what claims the title of an "event" and thus to exist must be such that it can be televised; it is and must be created, cut, limited by this inescapable demand whose essence we have recognized: the news (*actualité*). This refers to what is there now in its most extreme punctuality and superficiality – a superficiality and punctuality derived from its ability to be televised and from being televised – for the time that it will exist and after which it will fall into nothingness.

When political sociologism propels the content of society into the University, it is not only flooded with this content but also invaded with everything about media communication that enters into competition with the traditional mode of transmitting knowledge in the University. Repetition in contemporaneity is the essence of all authentic teaching, but it must give way to "the sciences of communication" which, under the guise of rethinking specific questions, ensures the general promotion of media communication: "True teaching is television!" And, with media communication, they also promote media existence. Surveys, opinion polls, what is talked about, stereotypes, general vulgarity, cartoons, the "new civilization of the image": all of this points back to banality and everyday prosaicism and is happily put on display. That is what professors subjugated to the news and social dogma are charged to teach. They have been changed into television viewers, who have become just as receptive and futile as them.

The concrete truth of this entire movement can be summed up as follows: *traditionally, intellectual and spiritual power was assumed by those who fulfilled the great movement of self-growth of life and who were dedicated to the task of transmitting it to others through a possible repetition, but this power has been taken away from the clerics and intellectuals by new masters who blindly serve the world of technology and the media – by journalists and politicians.*

But, then, what happens to culture and the humanity of the human being?

Notes

1   For a phenomenological description of this awakening of the body at the heart of the initial Parousia, one can refer to the poem by Guennadi Aïqui, "Le Cahier de Véronique" (Paris: Le Nouveau Commerce, 1984).

2   "Car les organs des sens ne nous rapportent rien de l'idée qui se reveille en nous à leur occasion, et ainsi cette idée a dû être en nous auparavant." Descartes, Lettre à Mersenne, July 22, 1642 in *Oeuvres III*, 418.

3   Sigmund Freud, *Gesammelte Werke*, vol X (London: Imago Publishing, 1991), 267. Change text that follows to: "The restriction "to the present time" is an amusing testimony of the refusal of scientific ideology to an unconditional capitulation to the apodictic evidence that scathingly denies it.

4   It goes without saying that the present critique is directed toward this "Galilean" sociology – but not against all possible sociology or even less against the Idea of it.

5   Karl Marx, *Oeuvres I* (Paris: Gallimard, 1963), 63

CONCLUSION: UNDERGROUND

Driven out of society by technological and media existence, and then out of the University itself (which has been invaded by the very same existence), culture is cast into a clandestine underground. There its nature and destination are changed completely, along with the society from which it has been excluded.

The key feature of modernity, which makes it into a barbarism of a hitherto unknown kind, is precisely to be a society lacking any culture and existing independently from it. As ordinary and common as it might seem today, this situation creates an almost untenable paradox, if it is the case that life, as self-conservation and self-growth, is itself a cultural process. This is something that all past civilizations illustrate. Barbarism is thus a sort of impossibility. If it happens nonetheless, it is never through an inexplicable dulling of the powers of life. Instead, the powers of life must be turned against themselves, in the phenomena of hate and resentment. This happens because life, in a suffering that is coextensive with its being and that it can no longer bear, attempts to get rid of itself. Barbarism cannot exist without the emergence of Evil, which is a mad but wholly intelligible desire for self-destruction. Or rather, in every state of social regression, it is possible to discover, underneath the evidence of the features of stagnation and decline, the violence of the deliberate refusal of life to be itself.

The nature of Western barbarism, and this is what gives it its great power, is that this refusal is not carried out against all forms of culture but within one of them: knowledge. We have seen how this happens. The project of gaining objective knowledge of the natural being led the founders of modernity to exclude all sensible and subjective properties from knowledge – they excluded everything that involved a reference to life. That is why the negation of life – that is to say, its self-negation –appeared to be a positive development, a development of knowledge and science. Concealed under the prestige of rigor, the putting out of play of subjectivity results in the devastation of the Earth by the a-subjective nature of technology. When applied to the knowledge of the human being, as in the case of the new "human sciences," it results in the pure and simple destruction of its humanity.

In spite of being cast out of the domain of knowledge, we have seen that life nonetheless remains in the form of brute needs. Today, this is what gives life its "materialistic" and barbarous character. Yet, inasmuch as every society is based on intersubjectivity, its basis is not just made up of the elementary ways of appeasing needs. Life implies a constant and ever-acting relationship among the subjectivities that comprise it. This essential interaction becomes possible in repetition and the contemporaneity that results from it. It does not take place initially as a deliberate mode of the transmission of knowledge in the higher forms of culture. Through the phenomena of intropathy and imitation, it occurs spontaneously as the very same process through which all concrete, pathetic intersubjectivity is self-constituted.

When this process is alienated by communication and the techno-media world, it adds an element of stupor to our materialistic society and at the same time strikes the final blow against culture. To justify the media world from which humanity is currently dying, it is customarily said that the media has always existed. After all, a Byzantine mosaic, a fresco, a book, an engraving, and the performance of a symphony are all media, and so culture itself is essentially media. These vulgar sophisms discreetly cover over the disgrace and hypocrisy of a society dedicated to the intellectual, moral and sensible debasement of its members and to a deep hatred of them. They would not have to be unmasked, if they were not repeated by those who can and therefore have the right to express themselves and who are all the creatures of the media.

The *media* of culture – mosaics, frescoes, engravings, books, music – usually had a sacred theme; in any case, their theme was the growth of life's powers up to the exalted discovery of its own essence. The *medium* was art, namely, the awakening of these powers with the aid of the sensibility that carries all the other ones. The ideal aesthetic image – whether visual or sonorous - was the object of contemplation. It was that which remained and that to which one always returned in the repetition of transcendental processes that led to its creation. To become their contemporary is precisely to reproduce these acts and increased powers of life within oneself. It is to reach them in and through the exaltation of the Basis (*Fonds*). Culture was the set of brilliant works that enabled and gave rise to this repetition – culture was the set of signs that human beings gave to one another through the centuries in order to surpass themselves.

The *media* of the technological age have very different characteristics. Their content is the Insignificant, the "news." Tomorrow it will no longer have the least interest. There is even good reason to believe that there is no interest at the time of the event. The *medium* is the televised image, instead of the permanent to which one must return in order to grow on one's own. It continually falls into a nothingness from which it will never be able to leave. The media world thus does not offer a self-realization of life; it offers escape. For all those whose laziness represses their energy and thus always leaves them discontent with themselves, it offers the opportunity to forget about their discontent. This forgetting recurs at each moment with each new rise of Force and Desire. Each weekend, students from the Parisian suburbs spend an average of twenty-one hours in front of their televisions, just like their teachers. At least they will have something to talk about the next day.

If one considers the great works of culture in terms of their transmission and thus as media, one must realize that their situation has changed. They were conceived in terms of their permanence and elevated to it. They were put forward in communication from themselves – from the ever-present and stable being of the temple, the fresco, or the book. They invested those who responded to them with the Sacred because they were its substance.

That is no longer the case today. Drowning in a flood of mass produced products, degrading advertisements of them, and televised images that continually follow one after another without interruption and then immediately disappear, "books" are no longer written by writers, thinkers, scholars, or artists. They are written by television hosts, politicians, singers, gangsters, prostitutes, sports stars, and adventurers of all kinds. The work of art no longer carries out its own promotion; it has ceased precisely to be the *medium*. It needs new media, an audio-visual intermediary that it never gets. The media is dependent on political authority (*l'instant politique*) as well as the reign and power of a social conformism that it feeds. In this way, the media depends on the dominant ideologies, fashions, and prevailing materialism. It also depends on a corruption through which communication seeks to become its own content. The media thus speaks primarily about the media. It announces what will happen there. It describes what has happened and will happen there. It also speaks about those who were and will be there, such as singers, actresses, politicians, adventurers, and sports stars. Those who are given a microphone are the new clerics, the true thinkers of our time. Along with them, there is the news, the always new and idiotic, the sensational and insignificant, the prevailing materialism, vulgarity, and the live broadcast. When thought is reduced to clichés and language to onomatopoeia, speech is given to those whose discourse is sure to be heard: the ones who know nothing and have nothing to say.

Because the media communication of the media world invades everything, values are henceforth the media's values. The fundamental and essential freedom - "the skeleton key to all the others" – is the freedom of the press, the freedom of information, that is to say, the freedom of the media and thus of the media world. In a radical sense, this is the unlimited freedom to stupefy, demean and enslave. For, there is yet another aspect of the media world. One lives an existence that is other than one's own, such that *the content that occupies one's mind is no longer produced by oneself but by the machine.* It takes care of everything by providing its images, hopes, fantasies, desires, and satisfactions. Though they are imaginary, they come to be the only satisfactions possible when the media world has become the real world. This society is not so much made up of social dependents as of mental dependents.

With the full development of the media world and its values, it is culture in general– which contrasts with it point by point – that is put out of play. We have already spoken about the absolute censorship. It is so merciless and radical that even the media is subjected to it. Determined by advertising, ratings, the iron law of the greatest number, and dumbing down, it wears the mask of democracy. In this chaotic parade of images that tear the human being away from itself, it has become almost impossible to introduce any production of another order, a true creation that would break the circle in which television and the public continually refer to one another with the reassuring image of their own mediocrity. That is what has been settled on by this censorship. Everything constituted within oneself as a fact or work of culture, as the process of the growth of a life in and through oneself, thus living from oneself and content to do so, is cast outside the media world, society, and the world that was once a human world.

What does culture become in this state? Its voice is never entirely silenced; it remains in the continual arrival of life within oneself. It remains in a sort of incognito. The exchange that it seeks no longer happens in the light of the City, through its monuments, paintings, music, education, and media. It has entered the clandestine. There are brief words, quick instructions, a few references that isolated individuals communicate to one another when, in chance meetings, they recognize themselves to be marked by the same sign. They would like to transmit this culture, to enable one to become what one is, and to escape the unbearable boredom of the techno-media world with its drugs, monstrous growth, and anonymous transcendence. But it has reduced them to silence once and for all. Can the world still be saved by some of them?

INDEX

Question what you thought before

Continuum Impacts - books that change the way we think

AESTHETIC THEORY – Theodor Adorno 9780826476913
ANTI-OEDIPUS – Gilles Deleuze & Félix Guattari 9780826476951
BERLIN ALEXANDERPLATZ – Alfred Döblin 9780826477897
CINEMA I – Gilles Deleuze 9780826477057
CINEMA II – Gilles Deleuze 9780826477064
THE CONFLICT OF INTERPRETATIONS – Paul Ricoeur 9780826477095
CRITICISM AND TRUTH – Roland Barthes 9780826477071
DECONSTRUCTION AND CRITICISM – Harold Bloom 9780826476920
DIFFERENCE AND REPETITION – Gilles Deleuze 9780826477156
DISCOURSE ON FREE WILL – Desiderius Eramus 9780826477941
DISSEMINATION – Jacques Derrida 9780826476968
THE DOCTRINE OF RECONCILIATION – Karl Barth 9780826477927
ECLIPSE OF REASON – Max Horkheimer 9780826477934
EDUCATION FOR CRITICAL CONSCIOUSNESS – Paolo Freire
   9780826477958
THE ESSENCE OF TRUTH – Martin Heidegger 9780826477040
AN ETHICS OF SEXUAL DIFFERENCE – Luce Irigaray 9780826477125
GOD IS NEW EACH MOMENT – Edward Schillebeeckx 9780826477019
I AND THOU – MARTIN BUBER 9780826476937
AN INTRODUCTION TO PHILOSOPHY – Jacques Maritain 9780826477170
JAZZ WRITINGS – Philip Larkin 9780826476999
LIBIDINAL ECONOMY – Jean-François Lyotard 9780826477002
LITERATURE, POLITICS AND CULTURE IN POSTWAR BRITAIN – Alan
   Sinfield 9780826477026
THE LOGIC OF SENSE – Gilles Deleuze 9780826477163
MARX'S CONCEPT OF MAN – Erich Fromm 9780826477910
MORAL MAN AND IMMORAL SOCIETY – Reinhold Niebuhr
   9780826477149
NIETZSCHE AND THE VICIOUS CIRCLE – Pierre Klossowski
   9780826477194
ON NIETZSCHE – George Bataille 9780826477088
PEDAGOGY OF HOPE – Paolo Freire 9780826477903
POSITIONS – Jacques Derrida 9780826477118
A THOUSAND PLATEAUS – Gilles Deleuze 9780826476944
TRUTH AND METHOD – Hans-Georg Gadamer 9780826476975
VIOLENCE AND THE SACRED – René Girard 9780826477187

Continuum Impacts
CHANGING MINDS

www.continuumbooks.com

CPSIA information can be obtained
at www.ICGtesting.com
Printed in the USA
LVHW021052181121
703703LV00009B/33

9 781441 132659